MW00447011

http://www.slatermuseum.org

Brainchild of the Reverend John Putnam Gulliver, Norwich Free Academy was founded by the wealthy industrialists of Norwich to provide a free education for not only their children, but those of all residents regardless of sex or condition. The original building, no longer extant, was designed by local architect, Evan Burdick, who also designed the Norwich Town Hall [pages 116 - 117]. A private institution, NFA today receives some municipal aid, but is independently administered. It is open to all who qualify, and has produced an abundance of notable graduates.

William Albert Slater [1857 – 1909] was graduated from NFA in 1875. His grant built and endowed the Slater Memorial Museum to honor his father, John Fox Slater, the wealthy industrialist who inherited the Slater Mill in Jewett City. [pages 174 - 175] William Albert Slater, steeped in European artistic tradition, retained Worcester architect Stephen Carpenter Earle to design his museum. In the Henry Hobson Richardson tradition, Earle has left us a stately edifice in the Romanesque Revival, or Richardson Romanesque style. The museum's intricate brickwork and soaring round tower leave a lasting impression.

The school's principal, Robert Porter Keep, convinced Albert Slater, in 1888, to further contribute to the Museum. Edwin Robinson, curator of Antiquities at Boston's Museum of Fine Arts, chose 227 statues from antiquity, and worked with Italian molder, Giovani Luchini, to assembly a gallery of classical sculpture representing the best of Greek, Roman, and Renaissance art. One can now wander a stately hall and gallery containing some of the most inspirational sculpture of western civilization – all this on a secondary school campus.

In 1906, a gift from Charles A. Converse enabled the Slater to add an art gallery that showcases the best work of both the school and the public.

The Slater Memorial Museum, open to all, continues its tradition of fine art, offering numerous classes to the many avid students attending Norwich Free Academy.

The companion volume to this:

Landmarks You Must Visit in Southeast Connecticut

Was published in 2010.

Many of the landmarks depicted therein complement those
of this volume
by their history, locale, or architecture.

I have referenced them in this book thus:
[LM page xx]
References without "LM" refer to this book.

Also by Constant Waterman

The Journals of Constant Waterman:
Paddling, Poling, and Sailing for the Love of it.

Moonwind at Large:
Sailing Hither and Yon

Vincus the Invisible Divulges His Secret Recipe for Maple
Pistachio Birch Beer Raspberry Ripple

Vincus the Invisible Visits Planet Earth

MORE
LANDMARKS

YOU MUST VISIT

In

SOUTHEAST CONNECTICUT

Constant Waterman (signature)

Written & illustrated
by
Constant Waterman

http://www.constantwaterman.com

MORE LANDMARKS YOU MUST VISIT IN SOUTHEAST CONNECTICUT

Text and illustrations copyright 2015
By
Matthew Goldman aka Constant Waterman

ISBN 978-0-9835288-4-5

Illustrations of Latham-Chester Store, Schooner *Mystic Whaler*, Hadlyme Public Hall, and H. L. Reynolds Co. appeared in my book, *Moonwind at Large*, published by Breakaway Books in 2012, and appear courtesy of my publisher, Garth Battista.

Author photo on back cover courtesy of my friend, John Wray

Cover layout and editing by
Marilena and Sandy Vaccaro
http://www.smart-graphics.com

Printed by Ingram Spark
http://www.ingramspark.com

First Edition

This volume is gratefully dedicated
to all of our Historical Societies,
who gallantly defend our past
from the depredations of Time.

ACKNOWLEDGEMENTS

wickipedia
mapquest.com
newlondonlandmarks.org
ctlandmarks.org
livingplaces.com/ct
historicbuildingsct.com
nlhistory.org
churchfinder.com
newenglandwaterfalls.com
national register of historic places
pequotmuseum.org
wpamurals.com – post office art
slatermuseum.org
stjamespoquetanuck.ctdiocese.org
roseledge.com
sites.google.com/sites/slaterlibrary
voluntownpeacetrust.org
great-awakening.com
lebanontownhall.org
dunhamwilcox.net   history of NL County – Norwich ecclesiastical history
ledyardsawmill.org
ct.gov/deep/cwp
mysticseaport.org
denisonhomestead.org
dpnc.org
bozrahchurch.org
naturesartvillage.com
conncoll.edu
fccnl
ocean-beach-park.com
thamesriverheritagepark.org
hikect.com

St. Clements – The Chronicle of a Connecticut River Castle. 1992
by Prudence Taylor Palmer & T. J. Palmer, AIA

New London Courthouse 1784 – 1984 by Weis Grube

Ivory business – article by Don Malcarne, Essex Historian

Julie Miller – NY Times – 29 Dec 1996 – American Velvet

thedistractedwanderer.com – Linda Orlomoski – Uncas Leap, etc.

History of New London, CT 1612-1860 – Frances M. Caulkins

Griswold – a History – Daniel L. Phillips – Tuttle, Morehouse, & Taylor 1929

Griswold in the 20th Century –
Ted Cyr & Erwin Goldstein – Hall & Bill Printing Co. 1999

"Elm Grove Cemetery Assoc. History," by Marilyn J. Comrie - 1981

Compilation on Daniel Packer Inne & Packer family by Charles Carroll Keeler

CT map:
Dept. of Economic & Community Development - www.ct.gov/ecd/cwp

"Latham Chester Store" by Marilyn Comrie – The [Mystic] Compass
4 May, 1988

Thanks to the libraries and historical societies of these towns and to:

Constance Kristofik, Executive Director of New London landmarks
Laurie M. Deredita, President of New London Landmarks
Leslie Evans, Director, Avery Copp Museum
Penny Parsekian, Chairman, Heritage Park Transition Team
Gail Kuster, Proprietor, Rose Ledge Country Inn & Farm Shoppe
Steve Manuel, Executive Director, New London County Historical Society
Klemens Zachhuber, Proprietor, Copper Beech Inn
Tom Bombria, Community Development Coordinator, City of New London
Rev. Timothy Dubeau, Pastor, the Congregational Church of Salem
Jane Reynolds Rowland DeWolf, Proprietor, H. L. Reynolds Store
Andrea Buka, Historian, Ledyard Library
Mary Anderson, Curator, Noank Historical Society

CONTENTS

INTRODUCTION

This, my second volume of Landmarks, covers all of New London County and a few towns about the mouth of the Connecticut. It's the companion volume of my first book, **Landmarks You Must Visit in Southeast Connecticut.** As some of these venues may change in function or become obsolete, it's important to document their present status for posterity. When you visit our area bring your sketch book or camera. Beautiful buildings and vistas abound – my books serve to whet your interest.

I could have made a book this size of only New London landmarks. Being a former county seat, it abounds in distinguished buildings. I've also introduced you to more rural communities. Attending a square dance or the annual art show at the Hadlyme Public Hall is certainly as rewarding as admiring the stately City Halls of Norwich and New London. Stopping at Reynolds Store by Hamburg Cove is a flash into the past. The 185' observation tower of the Pequot Museum thrust above the woods of rural Ledyard is a tribute to the centuries of civilization preceding the incursions of European culture.

As an illustrator, I always seek out structures of architectural interest to include. I get excited by steeples, turrets, arches, and leaded windows.I find the statuary at the Slater Museum inspirational, the building itself remarkable, and its history absorbing. See for yourself.

Nearly across the road from the Slater is a natural landmark, Uncas Leap, remarkable for its tale of valor and determination; for its waterfall and its trestles. Down the road a few miles pours aother natural wonder, Chapman Falls. A well-worn path to its foot testifies to the attraction of this cascading torrent of the Eight Mile River. Both are best enjoyed after a heavy rainfall.

As I haven't included every point of interest in the area, you'll have to delve further into the history of southeastern Connecticut. This entire region is known for lovely parks, art and antiques, museums, theaters, craft fairs, music, and eclectic dining. The venues I've depicted are only a sampling. Get out there and start exploring! I wish you joy and satisfaction in your searches.

Griswold, Connecticut
14 September, 2015

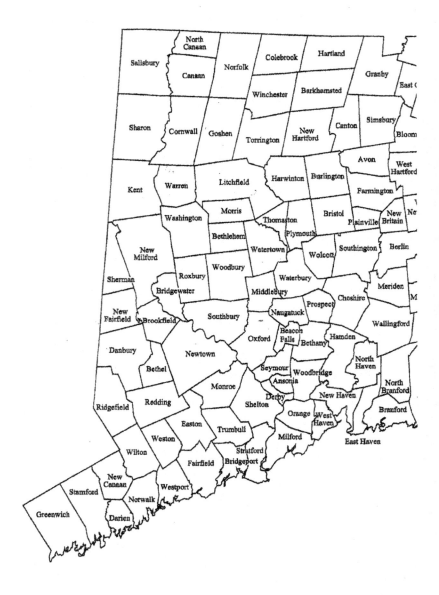

Connecticut Towns

Connecticut Department of Economic and Community Development 1996

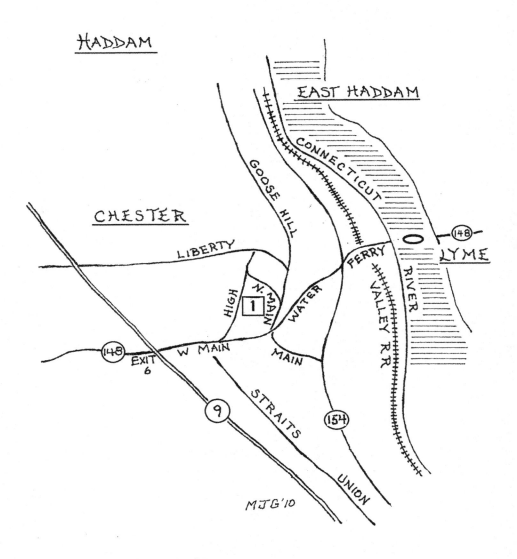

HADDAM

CHESTER

EAST HADDAM

DEEP RIVER

CHESTER

1   NORMA TERRIS THEATRE

NORMA TERRIS THEATRE
1984
33 North Main Street, Chester, CT 06412

Norma Terris [1904 – 1989] was born Norma Allison in Columbus, Kansas. After working as a vaudeville performer for Florenz Ziegfeld as an impersonator, she landed a star role in George M. Cohen's *Little Nellie Kelly*, and later created the role of Magnolia in Ziegfeld's 1927 production of *Showboat* by Jerome Kern and Oscar Hammerstein II. She afterwards made two films with Fox studios and starred for ten seasons with the Municipal Opera Company of St. Louis. By the 1940's she had become a patron of musical theater, and, later, was a trustee of the Goodspeed Opera House Foundation [LM cover & pg 1] in East Haddam, Connecticut for thirty years. In 1970 she performed in their production of *Little Mary Sunshine.* When the Goodspeed opened the Norma Terris Theatre in Chester, she presided over the 1984 dedication. In 1987 she founded the Norma Terris Fund dedicated to the improvement of musical theater. She passed away at her summer home in Lyme, Connecticut. She is remembered for her lovely voice, fine acting, and devoted patronage.

The Norma Terris Theatre is dedicated to the development of new musicals. It seats about 200 and has a flexible proscenium. It opened with a production of *Harrigan n' Hart* and has gone on to produce over eighty shows.

This old brick factory was built in the early nineteen hundreds for Susan Bates, Inc., a leading manufacturer of knitting needles and accessories. When the company moved to a larger facility nearby in 1982, they donated their old building to the Goodspeed Opera House Foundation in nearby East Haddam.

For more information visit both the Norma Terris and the Goodspeed Opera House at

http://www.goodspeed.org

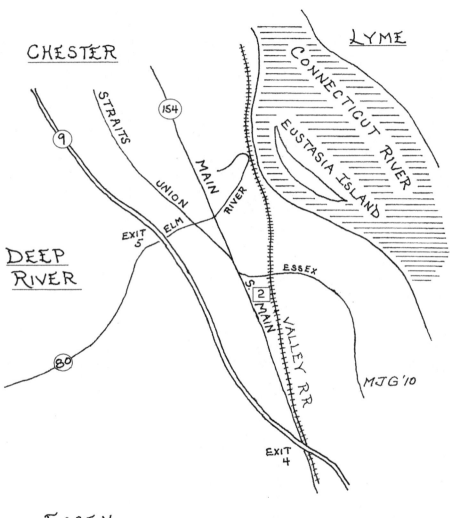

CHESTER

LYME

DEEP
RIVER

ESSEX

DEEP RIVER

2 THE STONE HOUSE

THE STONE HOUSE

1840

245 Main Street [CT route 154], Deep River, CT, 06417

Home to the Deep River Historical Society

http://www.deepriverhistoricalsociety.org

The Stone House was built of local granite in 1840 by Deacon Ezra Southworth as a home for his bride, Eunice Post. A plain gable roof was later constructed over the original, flat roof. Their son, Ezra Job Birney Southworth, married Fannie Shortland, and their daughter, Ada, was born here in 1882. The large two story wooden ell was added in 1881, and widened shortly after it was built. In 1899, the veranda was added along with the shingled dormer facing the street.

Ada married Charles N. Munson in 1906. Though they lived mostly in Jacksonville, Florida, Ada Southworth Munson eventually returned to Deep River, and lived in the house until her death in 1946. As she had no children, she left the *Stone House* to the historical society, which had been founded in 1937.

The *Stone House* has many unusual artifacts, including items manufactured locally from ivory before the age of plastics, and a piano built from the wood of the famed Charter Oak of Hartford – a 600 year old white oak, which fell in a storm in 1856. Connecticut's Charter, granted by Charles II in 1662, was in danger of being revoked by his successor, James II, in 1687. When the King's Governor General of New England, Sir Edmund Andros, came to seize it, the Colonists hid the charter in a hollow of this massive tree. An image of this oak adorns our Connecticut quarter, and several pieces of distinguished furniture, including our Governor's desk, were made from its wood.

Besides the furnishings of the house, The Society also maintains the Carriage House, which contains horse drawn vehicles on display, and a replica of a bleach house – a form of greenhouse used to bleach elephant ivory from its natural yellowish-brown to pristine white. Special exhibits at the Stone House can be found at their website and on Facebook.

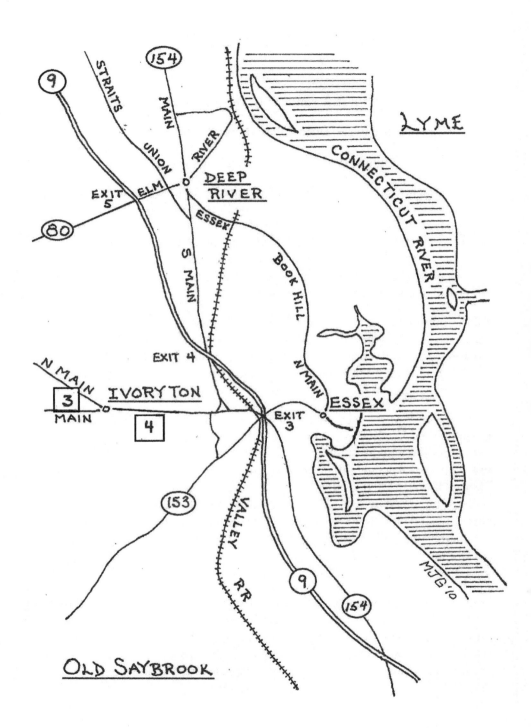

IVORYTON

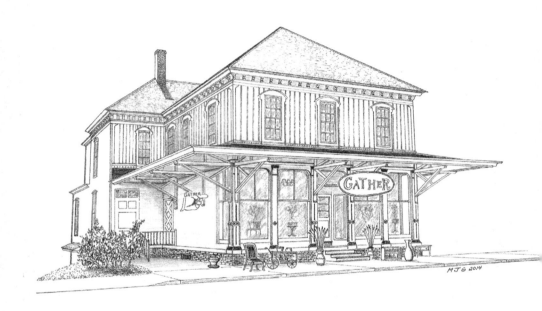

GATHER
104 Main Street, Ivoryton, CT 06442

http://www.gatherofivoryton.com

Samuel Merritt Comstock [1809 – 1878] began making ivory combs in 1834 using a machine invented during the 1790's by Deacon Phineas Pratt of Essex. Pratt and his descendants manufactured combs and other ivory products, eventually becoming the Pratt Reed Co. of Deep River.

The S. M. Comstock Company, organized in 1847, was located in Ivoryton – then known as West Centerbrook. In 1862 Comstock partnered with George A. Cheney, an ivory importer, to form Comstock, Cheney & Company. The business expanded – it now made billiard balls, combs, buttons, toothpicks, and dominoes, plus piano keys and piano actions.

Samuel's son, Archibald Welch Comstock, and George Cheney built a village to provide for their 700 employees. In addition to dormitories, the Ivoryton Public Library, still in existence, was built in 1889, partially funded by Comstock, Cheney, & Co. The Ivoryton Playhouse [LM 32-33] was built as a recreation hall in 1911.

This building I've depicted began as the general store in 1877. The upstairs, known as Comstock Hall, was rented by the Centerbrook Church – now the Ivoryton Congregational Church. Later known as Walt's Butcher Shop & Grocery & more recently as F. M. Rose General Store, this edifice now houses an emporium known as Gather – an eclectic purveyor of antiques, vintage apparel, houseware, gifts, homemade bread, cards, and memorabilia.

Deep River and Ivoryton accounted for at least 90% of all the ivory imported to this country. By the middle of the 19th century it was expected that every family own a piano or organ. The Great Depression of the 1930's adversely affected Comstock, Cheney & Co. In 1936 they merged with Pratt, Reed & Co. and gave up their name. After a brief resurgence of the piano business, World War II put a stop to the manufacture of pianos; Pratt, Reed & Co. produced wooden gliders for the war, employing 4,000 people in both towns. After the War, piano production resumed, somewhat stunted by the popularity of the Radio. In 1954, elephant ivory was banned by the US; soon plastic keys replaced ivory forever.

COPPER BEECH INN
1889
46 East Main Street, Ivoryton, CT 06442

http://www.copperbeechinnivoryton.com

In 1889, at the height of the ivory trade, when many families owned pianos or organs, Archibald Welsh Comstock, inheritor of his father's keyboard factory, built a large, luxurious house on 53 acres on East Main Street in Ivoryton.

Comstock, Cheney & Company, manufacturer of keyboards and piano actions, billiard balls, combs, and buttons, employed 700 people. The company built a village for them: a grammar school, library, general store, and dormitories. Later it would build them a recreation hall – now the Ivoryton Playhouse. The owners and administrators of the company built themselves grand houses along East Main Street – the Comstock house perhaps grandest of all.

On Archibald's death in 1940, his widow, Harriet, inherited their home. It was then appraised at $20,000 – a munificent sum. In 1954 the house was sold and turned into the Johnnycake Inn. By 1966 it had gone bankrupt. In 1972, on the verge of demolition, it was purchased by Robert and Jo McKenzie of Wethersfield, and again made into an inn and restaurant.

This time it derived its name from the enormous copper beech in front of the house. If you want to see this magnificent tree, don't put it off – it is gradually dying. Also don't put off your visit to the Copper Beech Inn – its classic charm, luxurious accommodations, and gourmet dining are worth the visit.

This four star inn is central to many points of interest: The Ivoryton Playhouse [LM 32-33], Goodspeed Opera House [LM cover], Norma Terrace Theater [16-17], Katherine Hepburn Theater & Cultural Center [30-31], Essex Steam Train [LM 30-31], Connecticut River Museum [LM 28-29], Gillette's Castle [LM 46-47], Chester-Hadlyme Ferry [LM 18-19], Chester Meeting House [LM 16-17], the Florence Griswold House [LM 64-65], and Lyme Art Association [LM 62-63].

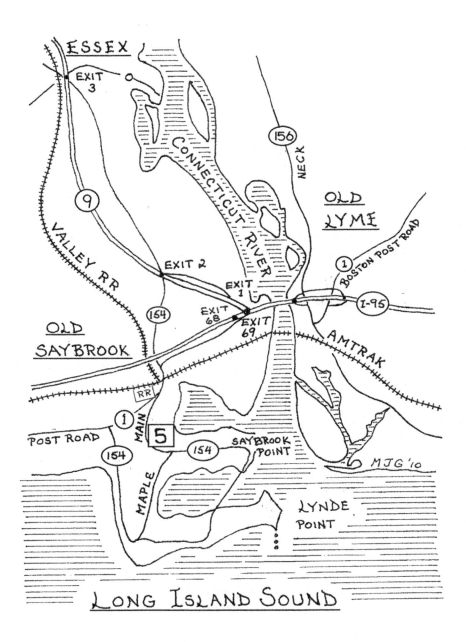

ESSEX

EXIT 3

156

NECK

OLD LYME

CONNECTICUT RIVER

9

VALLEY RR

EXIT 2

154

EXIT 1

1 BOSTON POST ROAD

EXIT 68

EXIT 69

I-95

OLD SAYBROOK

AMTRAK

RR

1

MAIN

POST ROAD

5

154

SAYBROOK POINT

154

MJG '10

MAPLE

LYNDE POINT

LONG ISLAND SOUND

OLD SAYBROOK

5   KATHERINE HEPBURN CULTURAL ARTS CENTER

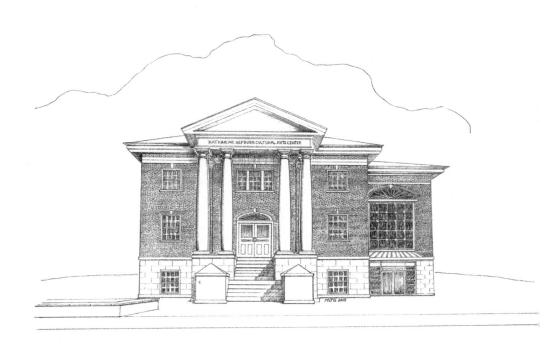

KATHARINE HEPBURN
CULTURAL ARTS CENTER

Built 1910 as Old Saybrook Town Hall

300 Main Street [CT route 154], Old Saybrook, CT, 06475

http://www.katharinehepburntheater.org

The acclaimed and controversial actress, Katharine Hepburn, [1907-2003] was Old Saybrook's most celebrated resident. A star of both stage and screen, she was the recipient of four Academy Awards for best actress, as well as another eight nominations. She was also nominated for Oscars, Emmy's, Golden Globes, Tony Awards, and others. She is a member of the American Theater Hall of Fame and a recipient of the Lifetime Achievement Award from the Screen Actors Guild. A serious and indefatigable worker at her profession, she set high standards for both stage and theater, as well as being an iconic model for women in her private life. She was not only handsome but active, athletic, and outspoken, albeit extremely private.

In 2009, Old Saybrook recognized her achievements by opening this cultural arts center to commemorate her life. It is the only such facility in existence at this time. It features a 250 seat theater and a small museum of photos, posters, and memorabilia of her career and life. Both public and private funds allowed the renovation of Old Saybrook's former town hall, built in 1910 and listed on the National Register of Historic Places in 2007. An example of Colonial Revival Style, it was designed by New London architect James Sweeney and built of red brick by contractor William L. Roe, Jr.

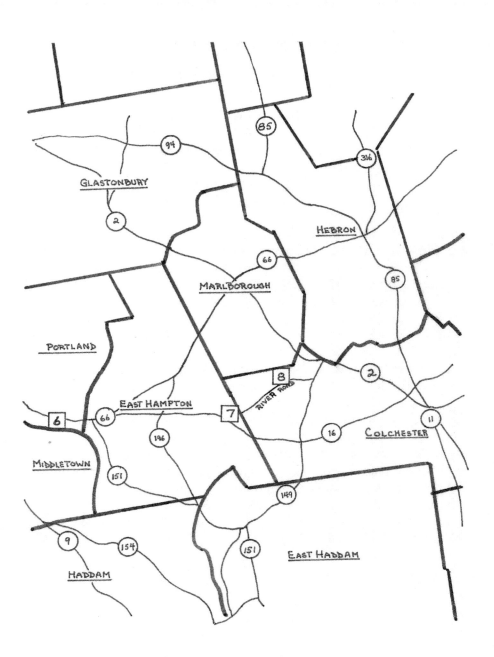

PORTLAND

6   **SAINT CLEMENTS CASTLE**

EAST HAMPTON

7   **COMSTOCK COVERED BRIDGE**

COLCHESTER

8   **AIRLINE RAILROAD BRIDGE**
        [RIVER ROAD OVERPASS]

SAINT CLEMENTS CASTLE
1902
1931 Portland-Cobalt Rd [CT route 66], Portland, CT 06480

http://www.saintclementscastle.com

In 1721 John Taylor moved to what was then known as East Middletown, which included Portland, Middle Haddam, and East Hampton – then known as Chatham. His great-grandson, Jeremiah, bought the center-hall farmhouse known as "The Hill," and began, in the 1820's, to acquire the land that eventually would extend to the Connecticut River.

In 1892, Jeremiah's grandson, Howard Augustus Taylor, a wealthy solicitor [1865–1920], married Gertrude Barnard Murray [1872–1928]. They determined to build a manor house overlooking a mile of the lovely Connecticut River. Its design was inspired by châteaux, manor houses, and inns the couple had visited in Normandy. It would be half timbered and stuccoed, with trefoil faced, overhung gable ends. There would be two towers: a stubby round structure with a conical roof at the eastern corner of the house, and an imposing, four story square tower at the main entrance.

They hired New York architect Algernon Sidney Bell and landscaper C. W. Leavitt, Jr., and began work in the autumn of 1901. A water conduit had to be laid from a spring far up the hill, and the long driveway, lined with chestnut trees, took as long to build as the house itself. The granite for the first story and towers came from nearby quarries; the chestnut timbers and planking were locally cut and sawn. Cyprus shakes protected the roof for 70 years.

The house was completed, except the square tower, 23 November 1902 – the birthday of Howard and the feast day of Pope Clement the First, later Saint Clement – patron saint of sailors. His statue resides over the entryway.

In 1968, Murray Taylor bequeathed the house with 92 acres to Wesleyan University. In 1993, Wesleyan gifted it to the Saint Clements Foundation, Inc. After careful restoration, the castle was opened to the public and made available as a banquet and conference center. It remains the most glamorous venue for a wedding on the lower Connecticut River.

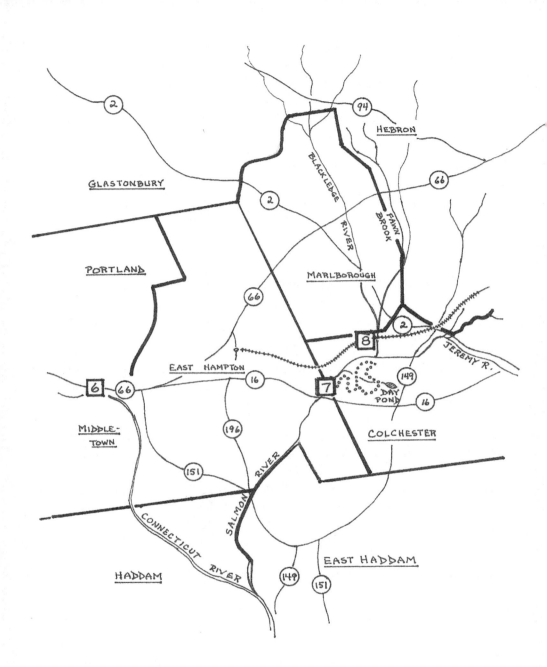

PORTLAND

6   SAINT CLEMENTS CASTLE

EAST HAMPTON

7   COMSTOCK COVERED BRIDGE

COLCHESTER

8   AIRLINE RAILROAD BRIDGE
[RIVER ROAD OVERPASS]

+++++   Rail trail

. . . . . .   Salmon River State Forest Trail

SALMON RIVER STATE FOREST
AIR LINE STATE PARK TRAIL
RIVER ROAD OVERPASS
DAY POND STATE PARK
COMSTOCK COVERED BRIDGE

By 1864 the Shoreline RR connected New York City and Boston, following a coastal route. In 1870 the Air Railway was laid out on a diagonal from New Haven to Boston to save time, eventually cutting an hour from the six hour Shoreline trip. It was named "Air Line" for the directness of its route, which resulted in the Air Line passing a dozen miles south of Hartford. By 1870 it had reached Middletown, and thence, via the new swing bridge across the Connecticut, to Portland. It passed through the Taylor property, and there was a small depot built in Middle Haddam – a short carriage drive away from both homesteads. Magnificent trestles were constructed: the Lyman Viaduct over Dickenson Creek in Colchester, Rapallo Viaduct over Flat Brook in E Hampton. As trains grew heavier and swifter, the magnificent trestles of the Air Line became unsafe. The curves and steep grades proved unsuitable. In 1898, the New Haven RR purchased the line, and though they reinforced the line they could not save it. Soon after, business began to revert to the Shore Line. In 1912, the two largest ravines of the Air Line, in East Hampton and Colchester, were filled in to reinforce the viaducts, but, by 1924, through service was terminated. Local service continued to decline. Heavy flooding in 1955 destroyed a major bridge in Putnam, which the financially strapped New Haven could not rebuild. More and more segments of the line were closed until the New Haven entered bankruptcy and, in 1970, was purchased by the Penn Central, who soon after closed the Air Line. A portion of the New Haven to Portland run is now occasionally employed by the Providence and Worcester short line, while the stretch from Franklin, Mass to Boston is now a part of the MBTA. Work continues on the intervening miles. The track has been removed and grading continues to make the Air Line State Park Trail more user friendly. It is hoped that it will one day become a part of the East Coast Greenway. **The Airline State Park Trail**, which originates at Watrous Street in East Hampton, also passes through **Salmon River State Forest**, whence it continues another fifty miles through the towns of Colchester, Hebron, Columbia, Lebanon, Windham, Chaplin, Hampton, Pomfret, Putnam, and Thompson. There is a break in the trail at Windham, and another between Putnam and Thompson. There are numerous access points

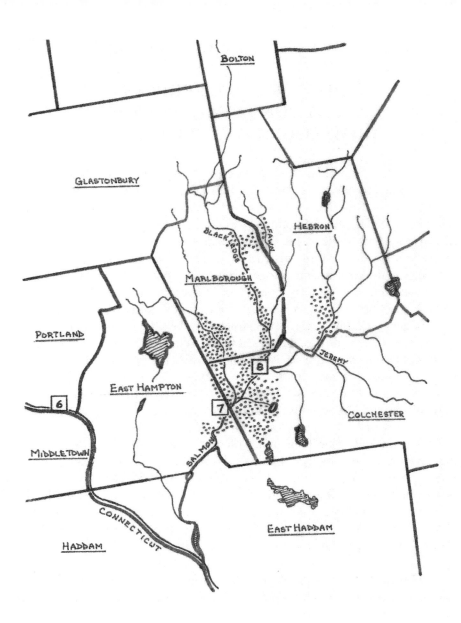

PORTLAND

6   SAINT CLEMENTS CASTLE

EAST HAMPTON

7   COMSTOCK COVERED BRIDGE

COLCHESTER

**8   AIRLINE RAILROAD BRIDGE
        [RIVER ROAD OVERPASS]**

::::: Salmon River State Forest

along its length. It is open to hikers, equestrians, bicyclists, cross country skiers, and leashed pets. Some stretches are ungraded, but the portion through East Hampton and Colchester is well maintained and suitable for wheelchair use. The **River Road Overpass**, pictured here, was added to the National Register of Historic places in 1986. It is only two miles above the **Comstock Covered Bridge** [accessible from CT Route 16].

Salmon River begins in Colchester at the confluence of the Blackledge River, which originates in Bolton, and the larger, though shorter Jeremy River, which begins in Hebron. The Salmon River separates Colchester and East Hampton, then East Haddam and Haddam Neck, and empties into the Connecticut, at a public landing. The Salmon River is known for its fishing, kayaking, and canoeing. On the Colchester side there is a seven mile hiking trail through **Salmon River State Forest**, much of it along the river. It begins at the **Comstock Covered Bridge,** and, at its farther end, loops by **Day Pond** - a lovely place to picnic, swim, and fish, with fire pits, a public beach, and changing rooms. It is accessible from CT route 149, which runs between route 16 and route 2.

The **Comstock Covered Bridge**, built in 1873 by the adjoining towns of East Hampton and Colchester, was not the first span across the Salmon River at this point. Another bridge preceded our Revolution, and was probably rebuilt numerous times. Earlier bridges were simple 'queen post trusses' – observable in smaller barn construction – and required piers in the river to help support the span. In 1840, William Howe, a carpenter and builder from Massachusetts, was granted a patent for his "Howe Truss'- incorporating vertical iron rods in tension between the roof and the deck, supplemented by diagonal wooden beams in compression to distribute the load back to distant piers. This design enables the Comstock Bridge to span the eighty feet between two piers. The roof protects the deck from rot, prevents the accumulation of snow, and gives shelter to travelers during storms. The bridge was overhauled in the 1930's by the Civilian Conservation Corps, reroofed in the 1970's, and received additional repairs in 2011.

The bridge was likely named for the brothers Christopher and Abner Comstock, who owned a sawmill not far upstream from the present bridge. The community around the mill was known as 'Comstock Bridge,' and even had its own post office for a while. The present bridge is closed to vehicular traffic. It was added to the National Register of Historic places in 1976.

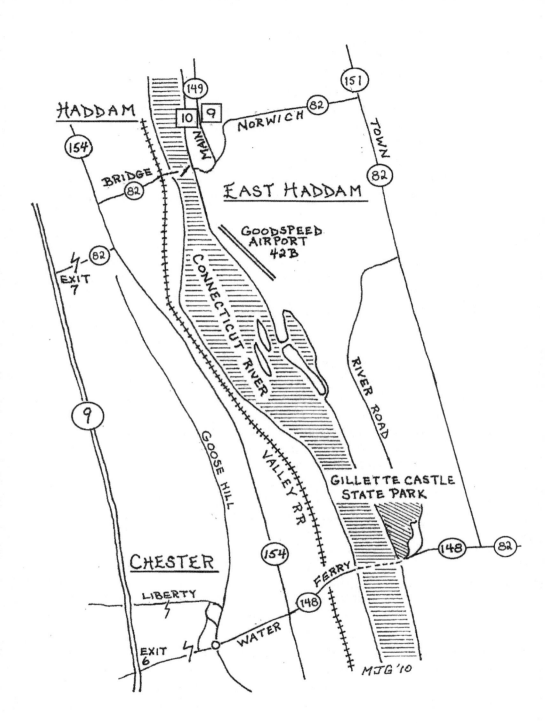

EAST HADDAM

RATHBUN FREE MEMORIAL LIBRARY
1935
36 Main Street [CT route 149], East Haddam, CT 06423

http://www.rathbun.lioninc.org

Libraries Online, Incorporated [LION or lioninc] is a consortium of Connecticut libraries dedicated to improving their services through electronic technology. At this time LION includes at least three dozen libraries, the Rathbun and East Haddam libraries being among them. At http://www.librarytechnology.org you can find technical data about the systems linking the data bases of member libraries. At http://www.libraries.org you can find directories of libraries worldwide.

The Rathbun was endowed by the generosity of Norris Wheeler Rathbun [1858 – 1922] and his wife, Frances Lavinia Emmons Rathbun [1860 – 1930]. N. W. Rathbun farmed in Millington – a village of East Haddam – where he grew hundreds of peach trees. He was also a justice of the peace, served on the local school committee, and was East Haddam's representative to the Connecticut General Assembly. He left an endowment of $200,000 to build and maintain a library for his town. Lavinia Emmons grew up in East Haddam, and left a legacy of $10,000 for the purchase of books. The Rathbun Library now has over 23,000 of them, and, partnered with the East Haddam Free Public Library in the village of Moodus, serves this town of 8,800 people.

The Rathbun Library, a Colonial Revival edifice of red brick, was completed by builders Whattams & May in 1935, and featured a long, gable ended room having a fireplace at either end. One of my early memories was of being curled up in a wing back chair in front of a fire, reading "The Wind in the Willows" as my mother assisted the librarian. The space downstairs served as a meeting room for various groups until 1991 when it was converted to the children's library. The impressive portraits of Norris and Lavinia Rathbun above their respective fireplaces were painted by the eminent local artist, Langdon Kihn.

St. STEPHENS EPISCOPAL CHURCH
1890

31 Main Street [CT route 149], East Haddam, CT 06423

http://www.ststeves.org

The first Episcopal service in East Haddam was performed by the Reverend Ebenezer Punderson in 1750. The present Episcopal Society began in 1791 when thirty-two disgruntled members of the First Church of Christ decided to build a more local edifice for their worship nearer East Haddam Landing. By 1795 an Episcopal Church of Colonial Meeting House Style had been erected on Porges Road overlooking the Connecticut River. It is believed that this is the last church consecrated by local Bishop Samuel Seabury. This building served for a century, after which time Judge Julius Attwood offered his Episcopal congregation a parcel of land to construct the present church. This church abuts the older Riverview cemetery.

On May 1, 1890, the new church was consecrated. It is built of local fieldstone in a style that is known as Shingle and Gothic Revival. It features lancets, quatre-foils, and friezes. Within, its hammer beams and paneling are attractive, as are its stained glass windows, the most prominent of which depicts the martyr, Saint Stephen.

The belfry at the rear of the church features the oldest bell in the New World. It was cast for a Spanish monastery in 815 AD, and used to ring the quarter hours. When Napoleon invaded Spain, the monastery church was destroyed. The bell was possibly brought to England by the Duke of Wellington after his defeat of Spain. In 1834, an American sea captain used the bell as part of his scrap metal ballast on his return voyage to New York. A local ship chandler sent it to his wife's hometown – East Haddam, Connecticut. It served in the first Episcopal Church and was transferred to the present church in 1904. Its controversial history can be read about at their website.

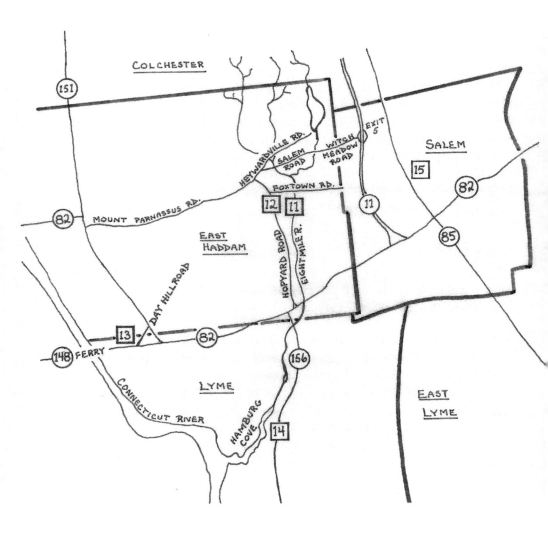

COLCHESTER

151

COLCHESTER

SALEM

EXIT 5

15

82

HEYWARDVILLE RD.

SALEM ROAD

WITCH MEADOW ROAD

FOXTOWN RD.

82   MOUNT PARNASSUS RD.

12   11

11

85

EAST HADDAM

HOPYARD ROAD

EIGHT MILE R.

DAY HILL ROAD

13

82

148 FERRY

156

CONNECTICUT RIVER

LYME

EAST LYME

HAMBURG COVE

14

50

EAST HADDAM
DEVIL'S HOPYARD STATE PARK

11   CHAPMAN FALLS
12   WPA BRIDGE #1603

LYME
13   HADLYME PUBLIC HALL
14   REYNOLDS STORE

SALEM
15   SALEM TOWN HOUSE

DEVIL'S HOPYARD STATE PARK
366 Hopyard Road, East Haddam, CT 06423

http://www.stateparks.com/devils_hopyard.html

In 1919, the former State Park and Forest Commission obtained an 860 acre parcel – over a square mile - located in the Millington section of East Haddam. The principle feature of the park, Chapman Falls, drops more than sixty feet over a series of steps in a Scotland Schist stone formation. The falls are a section of the Eight Mile River that once powered Beebe's Mills just upstream. These mills operated until the mid-1890's. For more information on the Eight Mile River Watershed please see my other book of local history: '**Landmarks You Must Visit in Southeast Connecticut**.' [LM 48 – 55]

The origin of the name "Devil's Hopyard" is lost to us. Hops were grown in this area, but the Devil was seldom encountered. Some thought this Gentleman responsible for the potholes churned in the face of the cliff beneath the tumbling waters. These perfectly cylindrical, smooth holes are caused by a back eddy swirling loose rock around and around for centuries – grinding deep depressions in the solid rock.

The Hopyard is a wonderful place to picnic, camp, hike, fish, and cross country ski, or just to meander leisurely and enjoy. There is a tiny covered bridge across the river – little more than a brook – twenty-one camp sites, and extensive trails. You should bring a camera or sketch book, as Chapman Falls is well worth your attentions. After several days of heavy rain they are truly impressive - thundering over the rocks, and casting spray and rainbows over the river. The bird watching here is especially good.

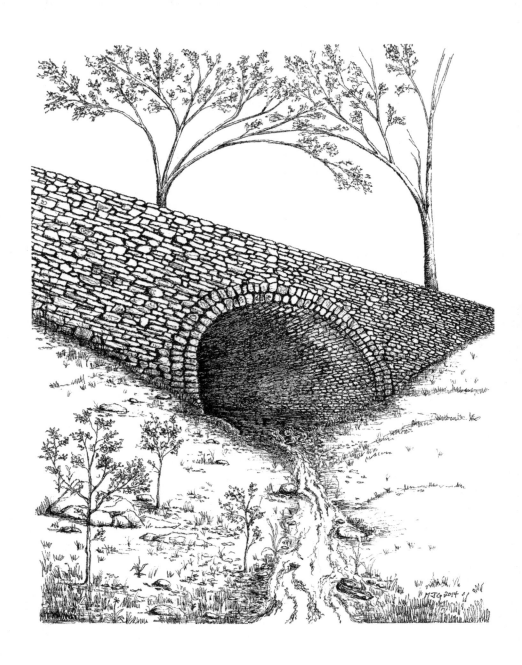

In 1937, the Works Progress Administration built three arched stone bridges along the Hopyard Road within the park. In 1993 they were listed with the National Register of Historic Places as bridges # 1603 [shown here], 1604, and 1605. They can also be found at http://www.bridgehunter.com and in the National Bridge Inventory.

HADLYME PUBLIC HALL
1911
1 Day Hill Road & CT route 148, Hadlyme, CT 06439

http://www.hadlymehall.com

The village of Hadlyme is another of our local anomalies – a village divided by two townships – East Haddam and Lyme. Hence the name. I grew up in the East Haddam portion and attended the East Haddam School; belonged to the East Haddam Boy Scouts and East Haddam Little League. Until the 1930's, students attended one room schoolhouses: either the Hadlyme North School in East Haddam, or the Hadlyme South School in Lyme. But the Hadlyme Public Hall, in Lyme, is used by people from both towns, as are the Hadlyme Post Office, Hadlyme Market, and the Chester – Hadlyme Ferry – also in Lyme – and the Hadlyme Church – in East Haddam. Growing up, I always attended the annual Halloween party at the Public Hall.

There were often square dances held at the Hall, and pot luck suppers, and my mother directed two one act plays in which my sister and I performed. In those days there was a ticket booth at the front of the Hall – it has since been sacrificed for the extra space. Though access to the upstairs is mainly the broad staircase shown, there is also a handicapped ramp on the right hand side. The hall is laid out with a raised stage upstairs across the back wall. A passageway beside it leads to a staircase down to the bathrooms, kitchen and dining area – each also accessible from outside. The open ceiling upstairs and the large windows create a sense of spaciousness in this little building.

Nowadays, there are still dances, suppers, music, and historical events. Continuing from 2002 is the annual art show beginning the Friday following Thanksgiving, and lasting the weekend. It features local artists - though some have gained a wider fame. Upstairs is art – and often music upon the stage; downstairs are crafts, and an almost continuous array of snacks served from the bustling kitchen. The modest commission taken by the Hall ensures its continuance – a grand thing for all of us.

H. L. REYNOLDS Co. General Store
1859

254-264 Hamburg Road [CT Route 156], Lyme, CT 06371

http://www.reynolds1859.com/history.html

For six generations the Reynolds family has operated businesses at Hamburg Cove in the town of Lyme. Beginning in 1859, Ephraim Otis Reynolds ran a shop building carriages. He also had a general store that sold grain, hardware, kerosene tanks, and other necessities. When wagon production proved unproductive, Ephraim changed over to a repair shop. His son Hayden Lord Reynolds took over in 1909 and changed the name of the store to H. L. Reynolds Co.

When automobiles usurped the carriage trade about 1915, one of Hayden's sons, Donald, began to repair the cars. About this time, he opened a marina behind the garage. In 1924, the present stone garage was constructed. Reynolds' Garage began to sell and service Durants, Fords, Chevrolets, and Studebakers. In 1936, the first marina building was erected. Donald's son, Leland, took over both the marina and the garage. In 1946 he acquired the first direct agency from Studebaker. In 1964 he became a Land Rover dealer. When Land Rover went out of business in 1974, Leland was already a dealer for Peugeot. Leland's son, Gary, sold Peugeots until 1992. By this time he had become a Subaru dealer. His three children, Kathryn, Tom, and Hayden, now own and operate Reynolds' Garage and Marine – recently voted the number one Subaru dealership in the country. The marina has flourished as well, and is presently a dealership for Yamaha and Mercury motors and a number of power boats.

Jane Reynolds Rowland DeWolf, great-granddaughter of Ephraim Otis Reynolds, has run the general store since 1953. Her collection of original art and prints is extensive. 'Jane's Dollhouses and Miniatures' became one more facet of a store that sold not only groceries, but toys, antiques, collectables, cards, and books. Her mother, Harriet Reynolds Rowland, was postmistress of the tiny postal office at the back of the shop. There were gas pumps and a kerosene tank in front of the store for years. All these are gone, yet the store remains. Dock your boat at Reynolds' Marine and walk up to 'Jane's' for an ice cream and a few memories.

SALEM TOWN HOUSE

1749

HOME TO THE SALEM HISTORICAL SOCIETY

270 Hartford Road [CT route 85], Salem, CT 06420

http://www. salemhistoricalsocietyct.org
http://www.cecnorwichct.org

Formerly "Christ Church in Chelsea," this small edifice stood on the site of the present Christ Episcopal Church on Washington Street in Norwich. During the Revolution the Episcopal Church – being an offshoot of the Anglican Church, and composed of many English sympathizers - fell into bad repute, despite having such distinguished followers as George Washington. During the War, parishioners held their services in secret at private houses.

After the Revolution, the Episcopalians moved this building to a more convenient location. It was enlarged and remodeled: a porch, steeple, and bell were added. It was rededicated by Connecticut's famous Bishop Seabury in 1791. In 1828, a brownstone church was erected on Church Street, and this little church became superfluous, and was sold to the Episcopal Society of Salem [formed in 1829] for $800. They disassembled it, moved it to its present location on the Salem green, and re-assembled it in 1831. The lancet windows and columned portico date from this reconstruction. A vaulted ceiling spans the entire interior space.

In 1848, Christ Church in Norwich built a new, brownstone house of worship on the original site at Washington Street. Part of the congregation refused to join them, formed the Trinity Parish, and remained at Church Street.

By 1843, the Episcopal Society of Salem became so inactive that they sold their church to the town for $500. The tower, spire, and pews were removed, and the church became the town hall – renamed "The Town House." The Episcopal Society was granted the use of it until they disbanded 10 years later. When Salem built a new town hall, the Salem Historical Society, founded in 1969, inherited the Town House.

The National Register of Historic Places included it in the Salem Historic District in 1980.

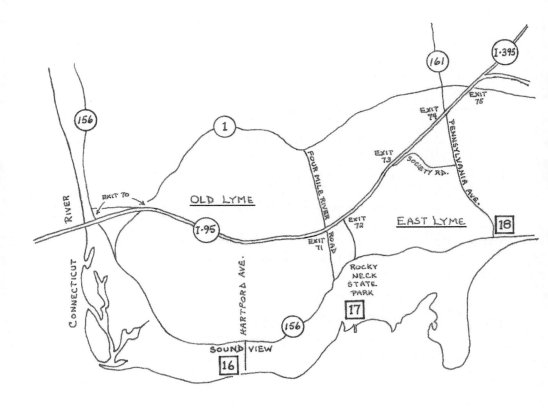

LONG ISLAND SOUND

OLD LYME

EAST LYME

CAROUSEL AT SOUND VIEW
1925

75 Hartford Avenue, Old Lyme, CT 06371

Sound View is a lovely town beach attended by small shops, restaurants, and one of the few carousels remaining in Connecticut. It is presently open from 7:00 - 9:00 in the evening from Memorial Day until Labor Day. This ride has horses meant only for children – 20 carved jumping horses and two stationery chariots. It is indoors and has an operating ring machine and musical accompaniment.

This carousel is designated a Country Fair Style half and half, meaning the horses are constructed with wooden bodies and aluminum heads and legs. It was built about 1925 by the Allan Herschell Company of North Tonawanda, New York, and was brought from Florida to Sound View in the late 1960's to replace the original carousel that dated from 1948.

The Vowels family, who has owned and operated it since 1987, also owns the two shops adjacent, which sell clothing, gifts, and 32 flavors of ice cream, yoghurt, and sherbet.

At the end of the 19th century there were over 3000 carousels in the United States. As of 2011 there were fewer than 200 antique wooden carousels remaining nationwide, though there are a number of newer reproductions. Connecticut has four antiques, including this one at Sound View; eight newer reproductions; and The New England Carousel Museum in Bristol. The Museum has created a carousel trail through Connecticut entitled *The Magnificent Carousels of Connecticut.* Also read : *The Carousel News and Trader Magazine.*

For locations and more information go to:
http://www.carouselnews.com

ELLIE MITCHELL PAVILION
1934
ROCKY NECK STATE PARK

244 West Main Street [CT route 156]
Niantic, CT 06357
I – 95 EXIT 72

In the nineteenth century, the land now comprising Rocky Neck State Park served as a dairy farm and a quarry. By 1852 a railway that followed the shoreline was constructed across the property. During the early twentieth century the land supported a fish oil factory that converted menhaden into oil and fertilizer by steaming the fish. The entire town of East Lyme enjoyed the pungent odor. By 1922 this company went out of business. A private campground followed. In 1931 the Connecticut General Assembly approved the purchase of 710 acres to be used as a state park. The pavilion was built in 1934 using the resources of the Works Progress Administration, Civilian Conservation Corps, and the Federal Emergency Relief Administration.

The Ellie Mitchell Pavilion is an impressive structure. Built of local cobblestone, it fronts Long Island Sound. Two generous storeys high, it stretches in a gentle curve for 356 feet, and is 80 feet wide. Within stand huge wooden pillars. It boasts eight fireplaces. The second floor is available to be rented for social functions and accommodates 300 people. The National Register of Historic Places listed the pavilion in 1986.

Rocky Neck State Park is known for its long and lovely beach where thousands come to bathe and tan, as well as a massive breakwater jutting out into the sea from which scores of fisherman can catch stripers, flounder, blackfish, and mackerel. The park has 160 campsites, concessions, showers and changing rooms, and acres of parking. There are numerous trails for walking and cycling, and salt marshes ideal for watching birds.

Please visit http://www.ct.gov/deep and click on 'parks and forests.'

THE OLD MORTON HOUSE
1868

215 Main Street [CT route 156], Niantic, CT, 06357

http://www.smartysniantic.com

The railroad brought immediate and positive change to our Connecticut shoreline. By 1851, the railroad brought visitors to the village of Niantic to enjoy the beaches, the boating, and the entertainment. Already, the nearby city of New London – known as a busy port – was realizing the advantages of speedy transport. Fish, whale oil, lumber, ice, textiles, and manufactured goods could be moved at hundreds of miles per day rather than dozens. Soon travelers began to appreciate the mere six hour journey connecting Boston to New York.

Niantic soon became a tourist town. Summer visitors needed hotels. The Second Empire portion of what we now know as the Morton House was begun in 1868 and completed in 1870 by Charles Beckwith of Hartford. Marcus Morton opened a restaurant in the hotel he named the Inca House. The hotel was also known as the Inca Inn and also as the Knickerbocker House. It became a popular venue for dining and dancing, for weddings and conventions. A pier with bath houses was built out into Niantic Bay. In 1884 a large addition doubled the size of the building.

In 1944 George and Athena Stavropoulos purchased the Morton House from Fred and Janet Rhomelin. It continued to flourish until the 1970's. Today the Old Morton House – or Morton Hotel – rents out 38 rooms on a long term basis. **Smarty's Pub**, at the west end of the building, provides good food in informal surroundings, a variety of libations, and musical entertainment. The large patio in front faces the ocean, and shaded tables add to your dining pleasure. Weekends during the summer feature live music outside. Their function room for parties, weddings, or conferences seats 75. This large yellow hotel cannot be missed.

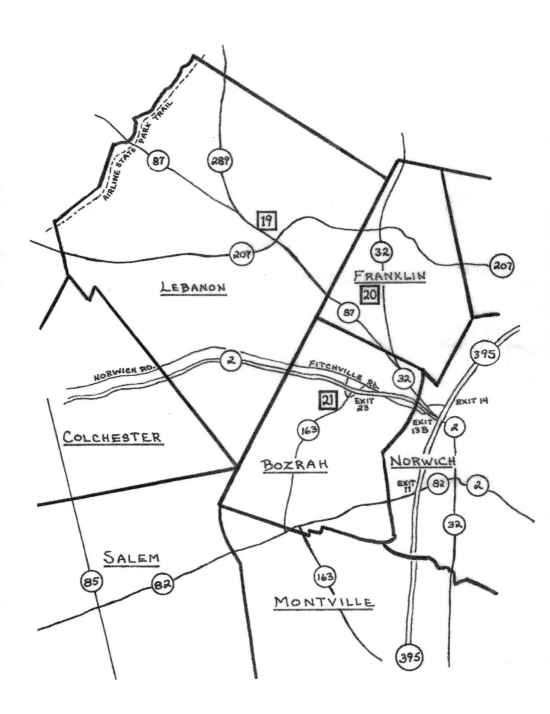

LEBANON

19   **JONATHAN TRUMBULL, JR. HOUSE MUSEUM**

FRANKLIN

20   **ASHBEL WOODWARD HOUSE MUSEUM**

BOZRAH

21   **BOZRAH CENTRE CONGREGATIONAL CHURCH**

- - - -   **Airline State Park Rail Trail**

JONATHAN TRUMBULL, Jr. HOUSE MUSEUM
1769
780 Trumbull Highway [CT route 87], Lebanon,, CT, 06249

http://www.lebanontownhall.org
http://www.historyoflebanon.org

National Register of Historic Places 1979

Jonathan Trumbull Junior [1740-1809], though often overshadowed by his famous father, the Revolutionary War governor, had a distinguished career of his own. After graduating from Harvard, he was active in business with his father and brothers, made trips to Nantucket for whale oil, managed the Trumbull flour mill in Lebanon, and supervised the Trumbull shipyard at East Haddam.

In 1775 Jonathan was appointed Paymaster General for the northern department of the Continental Army; in 1778 became the first Comptroller of the U.S. Treasury; in 1781, became military secretary to General Washington, and participated at the surrender of Cornwallis at Yorktown. A trusted friend and confidante of Washington, he accompanied him to the signing of the Treaty of Paris in 1783. Jonathan became a staunch nationalist and supported the Constitutional Convention of 1787. He was elected to the first U.S. Congress in 1789, and was later a U.S. Senator. In 1797 he was elected governor of Connecticut, and was reelected each year until his death in 1809.

His home on the Lebanon Green is distinguished by its interior hand carved paneling and corner fireplaces, produced by master carpenter Isaac Fitch, who also built the New London County Courthouse [pages 96 - 97].

The *Lebanon Green Historic District* has seven buildings worth seeing, one of which is the *Lebanon Historical Society Museum*. Another is *the War Office*, where General Washington, the Count de Rochambeau, and the Marquis de Lafayette, among others, met and planned. The French Army had their winter encampment and drilled their troops on the mile long Lebanon Green. This historic town has been aptly named the "Heartbeat of the Revolution."

73

ASHBEL WOODWARD HOUSE MUSEUM
1835

387 CT route 32, Franklin, CT, 06254

National Register of Historic Places 1992

This historic house museum is a fine example of Greek Revival architecture, having pedimented gables, pilasters at its corners and front entry way, and an entablature above the front door. It is sheathed in clapboard – presently painted slate blue – with white trim.

The house originally belonged to a local doctor, Ashbel Woodward, [1804-1885] who also served as surgeon with the 26th Connecticut Regiment during the Civil War. A native of Willington, CT, and a graduate of Bowdoin College, Dr. Woodward was also a local historian who published a number of papers. In addition, he ran a small farm – this property has two barns.

His descendants gave this property to the state in 1947, and it was later used by the Connecticut Department of Environmental Protection for wildlife studies. The state sold the house to the town of Franklin in 2000. It now serves as a local museum, and houses artifacts from Franklin's past.

BOZRAH CENTRE
CONGREGATIONAL CHURCH
1843

19 Bozrah Street [CT route 163], Bozrah, CT 06334

http://www.bozrahchurch.org

This white, Greek Revival-style meeting house stands on the west side of Bozrah Street and overlooks lovely Fitchville Pond.

"The Colonists who settled in what is now Southeastern Connecticut were Puritans at heart. Persecuted in England, they came to the New World to establish a Zion, determined to model their Church on the New Testament."

Bozrah Church was established in 1739 as the New Concord Society with Yale graduate, Reverend William Throop, as pastor. The first meeting house stood on the east side of Bozrah Street not far from the present Church. A larger one was built around 1770 on the west side, opposite the first one.

The present church was dedicated on October 25, 1843. The basement served as the Town Hall until 1947, when the Town deeded the church its share of the property. In 1872, Clarissa Haughton gave five adjoining acres for the present parsonage. In 2007 the fellowship hall and education building were added.

From their website: "In the Congregational tradition, Christ is the head of the Church, and all members are spiritually equal and called to the work of ministry. Each church is autonomous and complete. Believers bind themselves to one another in voluntary covenant. Every Christian possesses full liberty of conscience in interpreting the Gospel, and the Bible is a fully sufficient guide in matters of faith. It inspires individuals and directs the church with fresh truth for every generation."

Bozrah Centre Congregational Church and its parsonage were added to the National Register of Historic places in 1991. The church "epitomizes the antebellum New England Church structure."

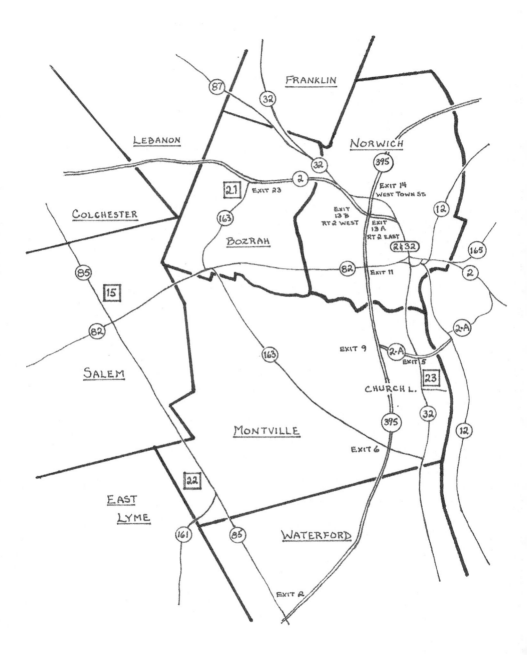

FRANKLIN

87

32

LEBANON

NORWICH

395

32

21 EXIT 23

EXIT 14
WEST TOWN ST.

COLCHESTER

163

EXIT
13 B
RT 2 WEST

EXIT
13 A
RT 2 EAST

12

BOZRAH

2&32

165

85

82 EXIT 11

2

15

82

163

2-A

SALEM

EXIT 9

2-A

EXIT 5

23

CHURCH L.

MONTVILLE

395

32

12

EXIT 6

22

EAST
LYME

161

85

WATERFORD

EXIT 2

SALEM

BOZRAH

MONTVILLE

NATURE'S ART VILLAGE
[THE DINOSAUR PLACE]
1991

1650 Hartford-New London Turnpike [CT route 85]
Montville, CT 06370

http://wwwnaturesartvillage.com

Beginning with a nearby shop that sold mostly minerals and crystals, *Nature's Art* has progressed to a large complex with 60 acres having over a mile of paths, 40 life-size replicas of Jurassic dinosaurs, and an amusement park for children, featuring a maze, a *Moon Bounce*, New England's largest *Splashpad*, and a climbing park. A seven acre pond lets you observe indigenous birds and wildlife.

The shop is filled with not only amazing crystals and minerals, but also fossils, replicas of fossils, statuary, toys, puzzles, books, jewelry, and more. Half of this shop is more a museum with displays and exhibits. One can sift for fossils and minerals; pan for gold; cut open geodes; learn about this Earth's remote past. For those who make your own jewelry, a huge room is dedicated to crystals, beads, and findings. Classes and books are available to improve your craft.

Another building houses *The Gateway Museum* of the much more recent past, displaying hand tools from the forge, the farm, and the waterfront, as well as boats, carriages, and antique machinery. *The PAST Antiques Marketplace* house over 90 vendors offering antiques and collectibles, and is touted by *Yankee Magazine*. A café offers lunch to the hungry collector; an ice cream shop fills in the empty corners.

This is an experience for the young, and the young at heart. Just keep your eyes open till you spot *Monty*, the Tyrannosaurus Rex who guards *The Dinosaur Place*. He stands just eight miles north of downtown New London. Be sure to visit their comprehensive website.

TANTAQUIDGEON INDIAN MUSEUM
MOHEGAN NATION
1819 Norwich – New London Turnpike [CT route 32]
****Turn at Church Lane****
Uncasville, CT 06382

http://www.mohegan.nsn.us

The Mohegan people originated in upstate New York, but migrated to Connecticut centuries ago. Uncas was the Connecticut sachem active during Colonial times. [see Uncas Leap, pages 114 - 115] Dr. Gladys Iola Tantaquidgeon [1899–2005], his descendent, ten generations removed, was an anthropologist and medicine woman of the Mohegan Nation. Her father, John, was sachem of his people. Although her early education in Uncasville was guided by the spiritualism and herbal lore of her people, Gladys went on to study anthropology at the University of Pennsylvania. Following extensive research she published her best known book, *Folk Medicine of the Delaware and Related Algonkian Indians*. With her father, John, and her brother, Harold, she co-founded the *Tantaquidgeon Indian Museum* in 1931. She worked with the Commissioner of Indian Affairs to promote Native American arts and traditions, and worked as librarian at the Niantic, CT woman's prison. From 1947 till 1998, she worked full time at the Tantaquidgeon Museum.

Her record keeping was instrumental in the federal government's recognition of the Mohegan Nation in 1994. She received honorary doctorate degrees from both the University of Connecticut and Yale University; membership in the Connecticut Womens Hall of Fame; the National Organization for Women's Harriet Tubman Award; and numerous other honors. She was elected Tribal Medicine Woman of the Mohegans in 1992.

She is remembered and revered for her dedication to civil rights, social justice, herbal lore, and Native American anthropology. She was an advocate, teacher, spiritual leader, traditionalist, and healer. Her legacy, and that of her people, is kept alive at this small museum in her native town. It is the oldest museum owned and operated by Native Americans. Her modest home still stands next door. You should also visit the attractive Mohegan Congregational Church just beyond the museum at 27 Church Lane.

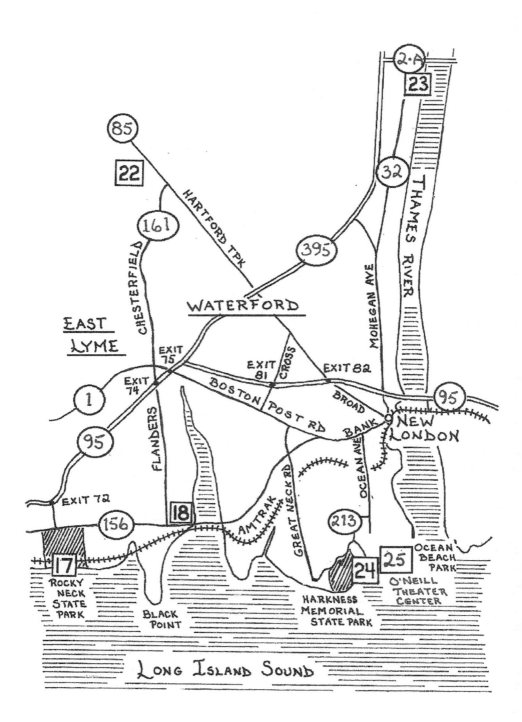

EAST LYME

MONTVILLE

WATERFORD

NEW LONDON

HAMMOND ESTATE
AKA
WALNUT GROVE

1822

305 Great Neck Road [CT route 213], Waterford, CT

http://www.theoneill.org

This stately manor house was begun by General William North [1755 – 1836], who admired the property from his yacht in 1820. In 1862 another wealthy visitor, Gardener Greene Hammond, [1835 – 1903] also viewed the property from his yacht. Under his ownership, the house was expanded, a third story added with a Mansard roof, and the gambrel roofed addition built at the back - the view shown here. The large ell has since been added. The house faces Long Island Sound across an expanse of meadows. A grove of large walnut trees formerly surrounded the house; huge copper beeches now adorn the back yard. Hammond built barns and outbuildings, and planted orchards and numerous trees about the 95 acres.

The property, henceforth known as the Hammond Estate, began as a summer residence, but the son, Edward Crowninshield Hammond, an industrialist and civic leader, lived in Waterford full time. In 1961, the town of Waterford purchased the estate to convert it to a park. Since 1964 they have leased the buildings and the 40 surrounding acres to the Eugene O'Neill Theater Center.

The vision of the O'Neill's founder, George C. White, has resulted in a nationally renowned venue for new theater. The National Playwrights' Conference, National Critics' Conference, National Musical Theater Conference, The Cabaret & Performance Conference, and the Puppetry Conference all make their homes here at Walnut Grove. National Theater for the Deaf and the National Theater Institute also resulted from the O'Neill.

Extensive restoration and the addition of an amphitheater and several buildings have resulted in a small but intensive campus for the performing arts. Numerous successes have ensured the continuance of this lovely property. See my article – LM 70-71.

OCEAN BEACH PARK

98 Neptune Avenue, New London, CT 06320

http://www.ocean-beach-park.com

Ocean Beach was developed at the end of the nineteenth century. The local trolley stopped here, and a covered pier accommodated small steamers. The Beach featured private cottages, and a dinner hall. The Hurricane of 1938 destroyed all this. During the 1940's the present park was constructed.

This comprises 50 acres, extensive parking, a half mile of boardwalk, a pristine sandy beach, and numerous attractions that keep both residents and vacationers returning year after year. Facing long Island Sound, one can see historic Ledge Lighthouse [LM 76-77] at the mouth of New London Harbor, and watch the massive car ferries ply the waters between New London and Orient Point, Fishers Island, and Block Island.

The Park features a 50 meter Olympic pool, an 18 hole miniature golf course, a water slide, a carousel, a Work Out World health club, playgrounds, and both a food court and banqueting hall for weddings or conferences. This hall has 8000 square feet and can accommodate up to 1200 people. A smaller facility is also available. There are snack and ice cream bars, a gift shop, an outdoor deck with a restaurant menu, changing rooms, video arcade, nature walk, and a spray park. There are. In short, there is something for everyone.

The Park operates from Memorial Day to Labor Day. Come swim in the sea, relax on the sand and enjoy the food.

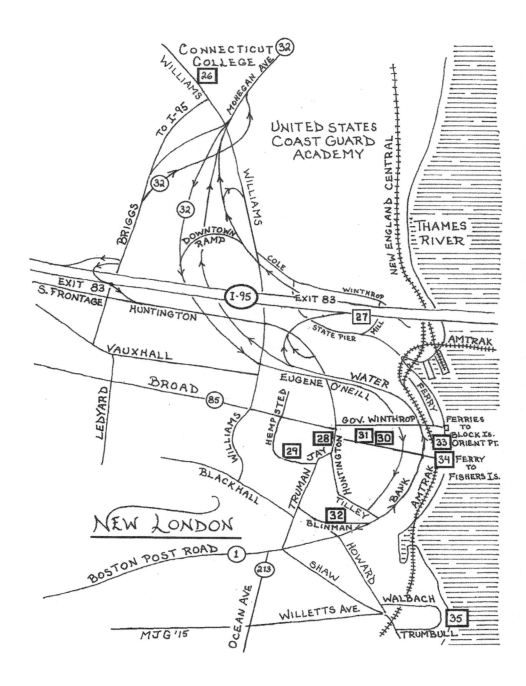

CONNECTICUT 32
COLLEGE 26

WILLIAMS
To I-95
MOHEGAN AVE.

UNITED STATES
COAST GUARD
ACADEMY

BRIGGS

32

32

WILLIAMS

DOWNTOWN
RAMP

COLE

NEW ENGLAND CENTRAL

THAMES
RIVER

EXIT 83
S. FRONTAGE

I-95

EXIT 83

WINTHROP

HUNTINGTON

27

STATE PIER

HILL

AMTRAK

VAUXHALL

BROAD

85

WILLIAMS

EUGENE O'NEILL

WATER

FERRY

LEDYARD

HEMPSTED

GOV. WINTHROP

FERRIES
TO
BLOCK Is.
ORIENT PT.

28

31

30

33

29

TRUMAN

JAY

HUNTINGTON

34

FERRY
TO
FISHERS Is.

BLACKHALL

TILLEY

BANK

AMTRAK

NEW LONDON

32

BLINMAN

BOSTON POST ROAD

1

213

SHAW

HOWARD

WALBACH

OCEAN AVE.

WILLETTS AVE.

TRUMBULL

35

MJG '15

NEW LONDON

26 HARKNESS CHAPEL

27 OLD TOWN MILL

28 NEW LONDON COUNTY COURTHOUSE

29 JOSHUA HEMPSTED HOUSE MUSEUM

30 MUNICIPAL BUILDING

31 FIRST CHURCH

32 SHAW-PERKINS MANSION

33 SCHOONER *MYSTIC WHALER*

34 NATIONAL COAST GUARD MUSEUM

35 USCG CUTTER *EAGLE*

HARKNESS CHAPEL

1918

CONNECTICUT COLLEGE

270 Mohegan Ave., New London, CT 06320

http://www.conncoll.edu

Mary Stillman Harkness, the daughter of a prominent New York lawyer and granddaughter of Thomas Greenman, a prosperous shipbuilder in Mystic, CT, married Edward S. Harkness (1874-1940), heir to part of the Standard Oil Co. Their summer home, *Eolia,* at the shore in Waterford, is now a Connecticut state park. [LM 72-73] The Harknesses contributed to the founding of Connecticut College in 1911. In addition to the chapel, Mrs. Harkness gave the College a residence hall - Mary Harkness House - and also made gifts for the infirmary and library.

James Gamble Rogers (1867-1947) was the architect. He is known for the classic "collegiate Gothic" buildings he designed for Yale, Northwestern and Columbia during the 1920s and '30s. He is appreciated for his sensitivity and attention to detail. Austin designed the organ in consultation with J. Lawrence Erb, the Connecticut College organist and professor of music from 1923-42. It has 47 speaking stops controlling 3,000 pipes.

Decorations on the ceiling of Harkness Chapel depict celestial, geometric and mythological themes. The artwork was done by George Davidson (1889-1965), who taught painting at Cooper Union Art School in New York and was a noted portrait artist. The chapel windows were made by G. Owen Bonawit (1891-1971), best known for his secular work, especially in libraries designed by Rogers at Yale and Northwestern. Twelve of the Harkness windows depict events in the life of Jesus.

The chapel bell is inscribed, "Great is truth and mighty above all things, [1Esdras 4:41.] The verse personifies truth as a woman of great strength. At the time the chapel was built Connecticut College admitted only women. The first men were enrolled in 1969.

OLD TOWN MILL
AKA
WINTHROP MILL
1650 REBUILT 1781

8 Mill Street, New London, CT, 06320

John Winthrop the Younger [1606 – 1676] was the son of John Winthrop, founder and first governor of the Massachusetts Bay Colony. He assisted his father at the Bay Colony, was governor of the new colony at Old Saybrook, and, in 1645, obtained title to lands in southeast Connecticut. In 1646 he founded that town first known as "Pequot," then as New London, and took up residence there in 1650. He was granted a monopoly on milling grain, as long as he or his heirs maintained ownership of the mill.

When Winthrop became Governor in 1657 he moved to Hartford, and leased the mill to James Rogers [1615-1687], a prosperous baker from Milford. Winthrop sold him land adjoining his mill where he built a stone house and bakery. Rogers supplied biscuit to the shipping industry of New London and to Colonial troops, among others.

Winthrop became magistrate of the Connecticut Colony as well as its governor. He united the New Haven Colony with Connecticut, admitted Quakers, and continued his scientific researches, which lead to his election as a Fellow of England's Royal Society. He was also one of the Commissioners of the Colonies of New England.

The mill remained in the Winthrop family until the late 18th century. When Benedict Arnold burned new London in 1781, at the end of the Revolution, he destroyed the mill. It was soon rebuilt, and went through numerous owners until 1892 when the city of New London acquired it and leased the milling rights till 1913. It was reconditioned in 1960 and placed on the National Register of Historic Places in 1982. The grounds are open to the public year round.

NEW LONDON COUNTY COURT HOUSE
1784
70 HUNTINGTON STREET, NEW LONDON, CT 06320

http://www.jud.ct.gov/external/kids/history/postcards/NLJD.htm

The first courthouse in New London – not yet the county seat – stood at the town square at Hempstead Street and Bulkley Place in the 17th century; the second near the Parade by the present railway station. On 6 September, 1781, Benedict Arnold burned much of New London including this courthouse. By 1784 a new building – essentially Colonial, but with Georgian overtones – had been constructed close to its present site.

Not in use until 1786, its first story remained unfinished until 1814. Nevertheless, many famous speakers – Thomas Paine, Daniel Webster, Horace Greeley, and the Marquis de Lafayette – orated here, and justice was meted out in many forms. In 1839 the building was moved back from the head of State Street to allow Huntington Street to continue to the north.

Originally designed by master carpenter Isaac Fitch of Lebanon – strongly recommended by then governor Jonathan Trumbull – the courthouse features a modified Dutch gambrel roof, a Palladian window above the entryway, and fluted pilasters beside the entry and at every corner.

In 1909, the courthouse received an addition – a main courtroom in back plus a law library. In 1984, the courthouse celebrated its bi-centennial. In 2011, a large addition saved it from extinction. In 2013 the building was rededicated. The New London Courthouse still serves as the Superior Court for New London County. It is the oldest courthouse in continuous use in Connecticut and one of the oldest courthouses in the country. It joined the National Register of Historic Places in 1970.

JOSHUA HEMPSTED HOUSE
1678
11 Hempsted Street, New London, CT 06320

http://www.ctlandmarks.org

The elder of the two Hempsted houses at this location was built by the father of the famous diarist, Joshua Hempsted II. The son lived his entire life here and kept a diary from 1711 until his death in 1758. In addition to keeping diaries that have proved invaluable to Colonial historians, the second Joshua Hempsted worked as a farmer, judge, gravestone carver, and shipwright.

Joshua, his wife, Abigail, and their nine children lived here. After her death in 1716, Joshua added an African-American slave, Adam Jackson, to the household. He also included some hired help, and raised two of his grandsons. An addition in 1728 housed his son, Nathaniel, and his family. The stone house adjacent was built in 1759 by Nathaniel, using Acadian labor. It is therefore also known as the Huguenot House.

Both these houses were spared by the British, who burned New London in 1781. The last Hempsted to live in Joshua's home was the famed poetess, Anna Hempsted Branch. Following her death in 1937, the house was purchased by the Connecticut Landmarks Society [Antiquarian & Landmarks Society, Inc. of CT]. During 1956 and 1957, restoration took place. The National Register of Historic Places listed the both Hempsted houses in 1970. They are also part of the Hempsted Historic District.

The Landmarks Society is careful to point out the 17th century portion of the house, with its diamond pane casement windows, and steeply pitched gable roof. The original house had the massive chimney at one end. The 18th century addition resulted in the house now having a central chimney. A huge fireplace for cooking faced the kitchen lean-to off the back.

MUNICIPAL BUILDING
1856
181 State Street, New London, CT 06320

http://www.historicbuildingsct.com

New London's City Hall, on State Street, was originally constructed in 1856 in a modest Italianate style. This nearly-square building then had a more residential appearance, in keeping with the houses that lined State Street in the mid-nineteenth century. The original design was by W.T. Hallett of Norwich, who also designed the imposing brick Baptist Church at 268 State Street, completed in the Romanesque-Revival style by 1856.

By the early twentieth century, however, large commercial buildings dominated the street and many in the city government wanted a more imposing Municipal Building to assert civic pride. City Hall was therefore substantially remodeled in 1912, upgraded to a Beaux-Arts, Neo-Classical design to be more in keeping with the surrounding architecture. The New London architect, James Sweeney, expanded the building in width and surrounded it by an imposing sheath of pale, grey granite having pedimented windows and Corinthian columns.

When you enter the lobby, you'll realize you have stepped back into the last century. When you climb the trodden marble steps to the second, tessellated floor, then to the third, you'll discover the City Council Committee room, having colorful murals on each of its walls. Next door is the City Council Chambers – an imposing lecture hall with coffered ceiling and tall, paired, white pilasters with gilded, Corinthian capitals. These date from the 1912 renovations.

Although barely adequate to the needs of New London, the Municipal Building has just received a grant for restoration – in a couple of years, a new elevator, new wiring, and restored ceilings will distinguish this stately building for the delectation of another generation.

The National Register of Historic Places included the Municipal Building in the Downtown New London Historic District in 1979.

FIRST CONGREGATIONAL CHURCH
[First Church of Christ]
1850
66 Union Street & State Street, New London, CT 06320

http://www.fccnl.org
http://www.churchfinder.com/churches/ct/new-london

Bringing European sensibilities to State Street, this Gothic Revival Church was designed by Leopold Eidlitz, who had trained in building construction at the Viennese Polytechnic, and later in the offices of Richard Upjohn in New York City. At that time, c. 1840, Upjohn was at work on the design of Trinity Church and Eidlitz learned construction methods of ecclesiastical structures. In 1850 while Eidlitz was working on the First Congregational Church, St. James Episcopal Church of New London, designed by Richard Upjohn, was under construction. As an architect Eidlitz went on to work in many styles. He also designed Harris Place at 165 State Street. In the late 1870s he collaborated with H. H. Richardson and F. L. Olmstead in the redesign of the New York State Capitol in Albany.

New London boasts several impressive houses of worship:

Congregation Beth El – 660 Ocean Avenue

Second Congregational – 45 Broad Street

St. James Episcopal – stained glass by Louis C. Tiffany – 76 Federal Street

Saint Mary Star of the Sea – 10 Huntington Street

First Baptist Church – 268 State Street

Apostolic Cathedral of Hope – 157 Green Street

New London Methodist Church – 130 Broad Street

Greek Orthodox Church – 200 Hempstead Street

SHAW-PERKINS MANSION
1756
11 Blinman Street, New London, CT 06320

Headquarters & Museum of the New London County Historical Society

Captain Nathaniel Shaw, who commanded vessels trading with Ireland, used the labor of Acadian refugees from Nova Scotia to cut granite from his property and build this Georgian style mansion. During the Revolution he hosted General George Washington, who was moving his army from Cambridge to New York. There is still a Washington Room upstairs. In 1824, the Shaws received the Marquis de Lafayette, who had aided the Colonists in their war of independence.

Nathaniel Shaw, Jr., First Selectman of New London, was named Naval Agent for Connecticut during the Revolution, and the mansion became Naval headquarters. Fifty privateers sailed out of New London harbor to harass the British fleet. In 1781, 1600 British troops under Benedict Arnold captured nearby Fort Trumbull and burned downtown New London. The Shaw Mansion barely escaped – a small fire was extinguished.

Five generations of Shaws and Perkins inhabited this home. The wooden wing on the right was replaced by one of granite during the life of Doctor Nathaniel Shaw Perkins. His daughter, Jane Shaw Perkins, was the last of the family to live here. In 1907 she sold the house to the New London County Historical Society to become their headquarters and museum. The National Register of Historic Places added the Shaw Mansion in 1970.

Find out more at http://www.nlhistory.org and on Facebook

SCHOONER *MYSTIC WHALER*

http://www.mysticwhalerfoundation.org
http://www.mysticwhalercruises.com
http://www.clearwater.org

This schooner is not, and was never a whaling ship. A reproduction of a nineteenth century coasting schooner for passengers, she was designed by Chubb Crocket of Camden, Maine and built in 1967 in Tarpon Springs, Florida. She was rebuilt in Providence, Rhode Island in 1993, and makes her home port in New London.

Her normal activities feature day sails as well as 2, 3, 4, and 5 day cruises in both Chesapeake Bay and Long Island Sound. She also participates in schooner races, tall ship events, the Connecticut Schooner Festival hosted by Mystic Seaport, and CT Maritime Heritage excursions. She also serves as auxiliary vessel to the sloop *Clearwater* on the Hudson River, showing her passengers how to keep our coastal waters clean. The Clearwater project was initiated by folk singer, environmentalist, and activist Pete Seeger in 1966 to educate people about the plight of the polluted Hudson River. The 106' sloop, *Clearwater*, is a school unto herself.

Mystic Whaler is the perfect vessel aboard which to combine learning and relaxing. Designed to carry 55 passengers for day sails or 34 overnight, she boasts modern conveniences, comfortable accommodations, and excellent food. There are lighthouse cruises, luncheon cruises, lobster dinner cruises, as well as overnights during which passengers can learn to set sail and steer this 110' schooner.

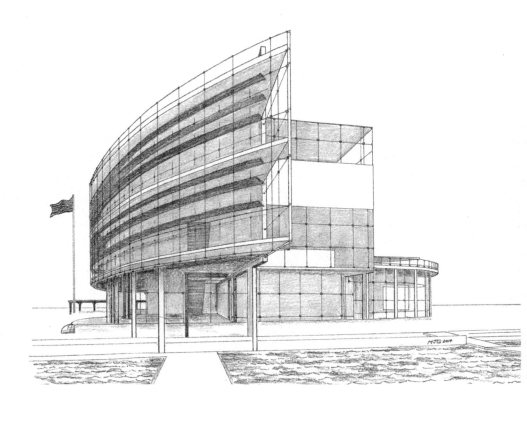

108

NATIONAL COAST GUARD MUSEUM

DUE TO OPEN 2018

Waterfront Park, New London, CT 06320

http://www.coastguardmuseum.org

Since 1790, the US Coast Guard has defended our coasts, maintained aids to navigation, rescued countless vessels in distress, and helped land troops during foreign invasions – from Normandy to Viet Nam. It is currently the only branch of our military without its own museum. Its founder, Alexander Hamilton, could not have conceived the scope of activities of the 42,000 men and women who dedicate their careers to our security.

It is only fitting that New London be chosen as the site of this commemorative monument to the Coast Guard. An old colony and important seaport, New London boasts the best harbor between New York and Boston. Here, the Coast Guard Academy trains future officers; here is the homeport of the magnificent barque, *Eagle* – our largest, active, square rigged ship with a national commission. Every cadet must spend some weeks aboard her, and she is known worldwide as America's tall ship.

The fact that Groton is also is home to the US Naval Submarine base, as well as Electric Boat, which builds submarines, makes this harbor a priority for coastal defense and security. Coast Guard cutters are stationed at the mouth of the Thames – harbor mouth to New London and Groton.

This new museum will inform the public of the extent of Coast Guard operations. Built with the sweeping curves of a ship, the Museum will stand by the bank of the Thames, affording the visitor magnificent views of the harbor, *Eagle,* and both lighthouses at the mouth of the river. Simulated rescues and storms at sea; interactive learning opportunities; and the extensive displays of USCG memorabilia will make this museum unique.

USCGC EAGLE [WIX-327]
1936
HOME PORT – NEW LONDON, CT

The 295' steel barque *Eagle* was built in Germany as one of four sail powered training vessels and launched under the name *Horst Wessel*. She continued as a training vessel until the end of World War II when she was surrendered to the British, and subsequently given to the United States as part of war reparations. She then replaced USCGC *Danmark* as the Coast Guard Academy's sixth training vessel, and the seventh Coast Guard cutter to bear her name. She is our only active, commissioned sailing ship in the US military.

Eagle has a permanent crew of seven officers and fifty enlisted. All cadets at the Academy spend a portion of their summers aboard, 150 at a time, to learn sailing, line handling, navigation, damage control, maintenance, seamanship, first aid, weather, and small boat handling. They stand watches, set sails, steer, and generally learn to work together to run a ship. They also learn leadership, discipline, and cooperation.

Eagle also represents the United States and the Coast Guard around the world. She is America's tall ship. Eagle attends tall ship and Op Sail events worldwide, and participates in festivals, regattas, races, and ceremonies.

She boasts a 1,000 hp Caterpillar Diesel that provides Eagle a cruising range under power alone of 5,450 miles at 7.5 knots, and a top speed of 10 knots. Her barque rig signifies her having square rig on her main and foremast, and fore and aft rig on her mizzen. Her sail plan equals 22,280 square feet, with which she has attained 19 knots on a broad reach – about 75 degrees off the true wind.

en.wickipedia.org/wicki/USCGC_Eagle_[WIX-327]

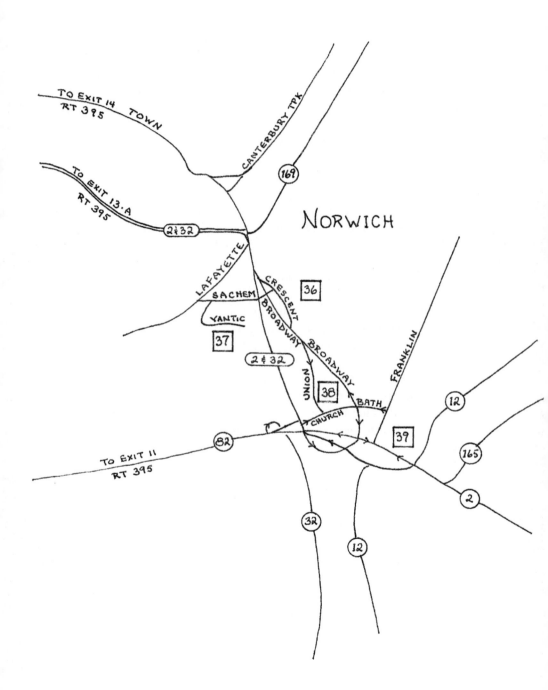

TO EXIT 14   TOWN
RT 395

CANTERBURY TPK

To EXIT 13-A
RT 395

2½32

169

NORWICH

LAFAYETTE

SACHEM

CRESCENT

BROADWAY

36

YANTIC

37

BROADWAY

2½32

UNION

38

BATH

FRANKLIN

12

82

CHURCH

39

165

To EXIT 11
RT 395

2

32

12

UNCAS LEAP

AKA

INDIAN LEAP

YANTIC RIVER

Yantic Street, Norwich, CT, 06360

http://www.newenglandwaterfalls.com

Uncas, Sachem of the Mohegans, led his outnumbered warriors against 900 of the Narragansetts at "The Battle of the Great Plain" in 1643. During the battle, the Narragansetts were pursued by the Mohegans. Many of Narragansetts, unfamiliar with the territory, found themselves at the precipitous gorge below the Falls. Rather than surrender, they attempted to leap the chasm. All fell to their deaths except their leader, Miantonomo, who made the leap and survived, though he hurt his leg. Uncas also made the terrific leap, then pursued and captured his injured enemy.

Uncas then brought Miantonomo to the Colonial Commissioners in Hartford and surrendered him to the English. The Commissioners ruled that Miantonomo should be executed, and gave him into the custody of Uncas. After dispatching his enemy, Uncas honored him by burying him beside the Shetucket River nearby the Falls, and erecting a commemorative marker. A modern marker was erected in 1841 and can be visited on Elijah Street off Boswell Ave. A monument to Uncas can be visited at the remains of the Mohegan burying ground on Sherman Street, near The Leap.

Since the seventeenth century the dam at Yantic Falls – the Lower Falls - has supplied power for a grist mill, paper making, a cotton mill, and a nail factory. A trestle of the New England Central RR crosses the river just above the Falls, and a foot bridge – ideal for observing Indian Leap - crosses beside it. Parking is available on Yantic Street. The dam, mill pond, and power house of the Upper Falls are just a short walk upstream in Upper Heritage Falls Park off Sherman Street where parking is also available.

NORWICH TOWN HALL
1870-1873
Union Street & Broadway, Norwich, CT 06415

This magnificent red-brick edifice is a noble example of the Second Empire architecture that proved influential in this country in the latter part of the nineteenth and into the early twentieth centuries. The Goodspeed Opera House in East Haddam [1876] [LM cover & pg 1], the Old Morton House in Niantic [1868] [pages 68 - 69], and Ledge Lighthouse at the mouth of the Thames River [1909] [LM 76-77] are other examples.

The Mansard roof and carved wooden trim attest to the time and effort to erect this building, which took three years to complete. The clock tower was added in 1909. The stately cast iron stair case and balustrade with its ornamentation is a work of art.

The architects were Burdick and Arnold. Arnold supervised the building; the contractor was John Murphy. The cost of the building in 1875 dollars was $315,000 – a stupendous amount of money in those days. When the staircase and balustrade were totally rebuilt in 2013, the cost was $347,000 – more than the original cost of the building.

The Town Hall stands at the junction of Broadway and Union streets facing Union Square. It is 110 feet deep, 108 feet wide, and 87' tall. The basement story, which originally housed the jail, is of cut granite, the roof is covered with tin. The tower contains a clock with illuminated dials, and a 3,000 pound bell, which is used by the clock and also acts as a fire alarm.

The National Register of Historic Places listed the Town Hall in 1983. It was also included in their downtown historic district listing in 1985.

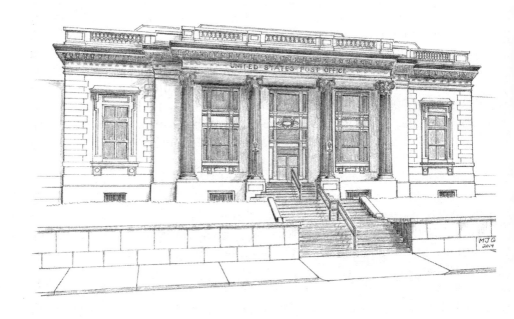

NORWICH POST OFFICE
1905
340 Main Street [CT route 2], Norwich, CT 06360

This classical revival post office of 23,000 square feet was designed by James Knox Taylor in 1903 and completed two years later. It has a steel frame with brick and limestone facing, a mansard roof surrounded by a stone balustrade, and Ionic columns.

During the Depression of the 1930's, New Deal Artwork hired artists to embellish public buildings. In 1934, the Treasury Department established the "Section of Painting and Sculpture," later known as the "Section of Fine Arts." It was administered by the Procurement Division of the Treasury under the leadership of Edward Bruce.

The Norwich Post Office is graced by a 1940 mural by George Kanelous entitled "Taking Up Arms - 1776" – a depiction of the Colonists arming themselves against the British. The other Post Office in our area that deserves attention is in New London, where a mural by Tom La Farge depicting the whaling industry adorns the lobby. For a listing of Post Office art throughout the country, visit http://www.wpamurals.com Although these commissions were not part of the Works Progress Administration, they appear as part of its website.

George Kanelous [1915-1998] was born in Uruguay of Greek parents but came to this country as a small child. His career included fine art, commercial illustration, and several murals for "New Deal Artwork," mostly in the Boston area. By the 1970's he was president of the Phoenix Gallery in New York City. You can find his artwork at http://www.kanelousdesign.com

The Norwich Post Office is currently in a precarious financial predicament and, recently, this stately building was for sale. The National Register of Historic Places added it in 1986. As of 1986, it was also included in the Historic Downtown Norwich District.

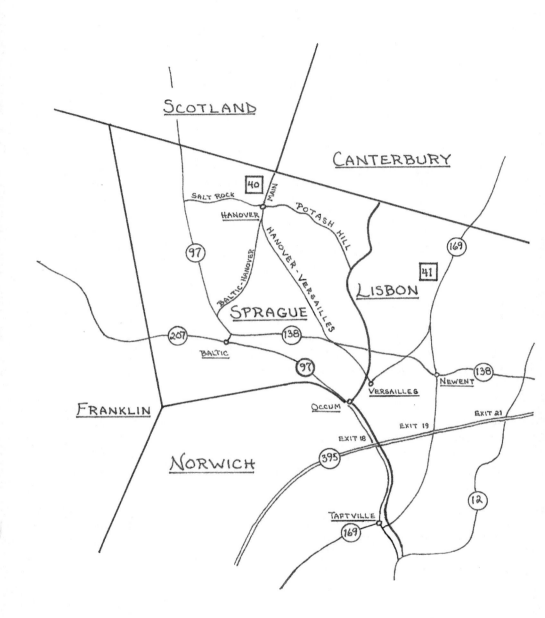

SPRAGUE

40   WILLIAM PARK HOUSE

LISBON

41   JOHN PALMER HOUSE

WILLIAM PARK HOUSE
1913
330 Main Street, Hanover, CT, 06350

PRIVATE RESIDENCE

National Register of Historic Places 2007

Angus Park purchased the defunct Allen Mill in Hanover – a village in Sprague – in 1899, and transformed it into the successful Airlie Woolen Mills, which operated until 1973. This house was a wedding gift for his son, William Park (1889-1971) at the time of his marriage to Ruth Standish.

This example of Bungalow/Craftsman and Prairie School Architecture was built, and probably designed, by master builder Peck McWilliams. Bungalow usually refers to a house having wide verandas, and a low, sloping roof, often with dormers. The Craftsman style usually referred to large overhangs and exposed rafters and a simplistic style of design.

The Prairie School of Architecture is just that: recent designs that reflect or compliment flat, open spaces. They generally have hipped or flatter roofs, rows or groupings of connected windows, and look as though they may have sprung from the prairie. Frank Lloyd Wright is the most famous proponent of this style. The Prairie School is a strictly American phenomenon and a clear break from the classic and neo-classic styles that came from Europe.

Both these styles incorporated in the Park House favor a handcrafted, rather than mass produced appearance, and reflect the simple elegance influenced by the teachings of William Morris and John Ruskin.

The Park House is rather unusual in this sedate New England village of white clapboard Colonials. It has walls with Tudor-style decorative half-timbering and a porte-cochere on the north side. It is a private residence and not open to the public; yet it deserves a drive by to admire its rustic grandeur. It is prominently set on a knoll surrounded by three acres of well-kept lawn.

JOHN PALMER HOUSE

1790

291 North Burnham Hwy. [CT route 169], Lisbon, CT 06351

National Register of Historic Places in 2005

The Palmer House is being restored to continue as a vineyard and café.

http://www.great-awakening.com

This house is significant for association with the Reverend John Palmer's involvement in the *First Great Awakening* - a religious revival championed by the British Evangelist, George White, and by the famous American theologian, Jonathan Edwards. John Palmer was a preacher and a Separatist leader from 1746 until his death c.1800.

The *First Great Awakening* began in the 1730s and lasted to about 1743. Four subsequent Awakenings are documented until the 1990's. Whitefield first arrived in Georgia in 1738, and subsequently visited most of the Eastern Colonies. His influence extended to the Maritime Provinces. Ministers from various evangelical Protestant denominations supported his teachings and his enormous following challenged the established Church. The Baptist Church profited greatly from this movement.

This revival was based on the emotional, rather than the intellectual response to Christian teachings, and on the premise that an uncontrolled sharing of information and an individual interpretation of the Bible were fundamental to salvation. This democratic interpretation of Christianity, including a belief in the free press, proved instrumental in creating not only a demand for religious freedom, but also freedom from oppression. It was embraced by both the African American slaves and by the Revolutionary Colonists. Joseph Tracy, minister, historian, and preacher, gave this religious phenomenon its name in his influential 1842 book, *The Great Awakening*. He saw the *First Great Awakening* as a precursor to the American Revolution.

Subsequent Awakenings have influenced the abolition of slavery and women's suffrage, and contributed to the establishment of Mormonism, the Seventh-day Adventist Church, and numerous other evangelical sects.

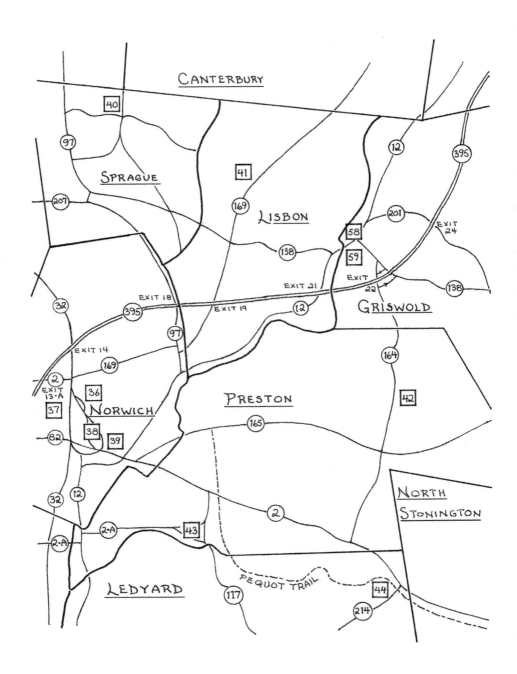

NORWICH

36 SLATER MUSEUM
37 UNCAS LEAP
38 NORWICH TOWN HALL
39 NORWICH POST OFFICE

SPRAGUE

40 WILLIAM PARK HOUSE

LISBON

41 JOHN PALMER HOUSE

PRESTON

42 ROSELEDGE COUNTRY INN

43 SAINT JAMES EPISCOPAL CHURCH

LEDYARD

44 MASHANTUCKET PEQUOT MUSEUM

GRISWOLD

58 SLATER LIBRARY
59 SLATER MILL & FLEA MARKET

- - - - Pequot hiking trail

ROSELEDGE COUNTRY INN & FARM SHOPPE
1994
Built 1720 as John Meech House
418 Route 164, Preston, CT 06365

http://www.roseledge.com

"Yankee Magazine Editors choice - Best of New England 2014"

This Colonial house is built on ledge and surrounded by roses – hence the name. It features a massive central chimney, stone tunnels through its cellar, and wide board floors. It is surrounded by beautiful herb and flower gardens, rugged stone walls, and venerable trees. It is a ceaseless labor of love for its indefatigable owner, innkeeper, cook, and avid gardener, Gail Kuster. The three rooms of this B & B have four poster beds, working fireplaces, and are graced daily by fresh cut flowers.

In addition to home cooked breakfast, afternoon snacks of home baked goods with cider or fresh lemonade are available to guests, and free wine is served in the evening. Homemade lunches and teas are available to both residents and the public by prior request, and may be enjoyed outside during clement weather. Stroll the gardens on flagstone paths or relax in a shady place.

For entertainment visit the nearby casinos – The Mohegan Sun, and Foxwoods. The Mashantucket Pequot Museum and the Mohegan's Tantaquidgeon Museum are also nearby. Mystic Aquarium, Mystic Seaport, Mystic Arts Center, Submarine Force Museum, Ocean Beach Park, Slater Museum, Lyman Allyn Art Museum, Hygienic Arts, Garde Arts, O'Neill Theater, Fort Griswold, Fort Trumbull, and the Customs House Maritime Museum are all a half hour's country drive. College Mart Flea Market is open every Sunday and is indoors, and the 18 hole River Ridge Golf course is just a couple of miles up the road. Wineries, corn mazes, and homemade ice cream are also nearby.

The Roseledge Farm Shoppe – open to the public - features dried herbs, sachets, herbal soaps, country gifts, and honey. A tasteful selection of potted herbs and flowers is available for sale. Come for a weekend, come for tea, come to visit the gardens, come to buy flowers!

SAINT JAMES EPISCOPAL CHURCH
1898
95 Route 2-A, Preston, CT 06365

http://www.stjamespoquetanuck.ctdiocese.org

During the 17th century the Church of England was scarcely tolerated in Connecticut, for the colony had been settled by dissenters from her doctrine, discipline and rites. In 1734 St. James' Parish was organized through the efforts of the Reverend Ebenezer Punderson Sr.[1708-1771], and the first church building was erected: a wooden-frame edifice, 40 feet by 60 feet, with galleries but no steeple. It was at the back of the property, with a graveyard in the front. The original blueprint site is still obvious, with graves and markers, at the top of Spicer Hill Road (formerly Church Hill Road) in Ledyard. In 1785 the church was moved to Shingle Point Road in Ledyard, just south of the head of Poquetanuck Cove, and adjacent to the Town of Preston. At the new site Samuel Seabury served the parish from 1784 through 1794.

In 1840 a handsome Greek Revival Church was built at the current site, soon followed by the present church - occupied on Good Friday - April 8, 1898. It had a three paned Chancel Window of leaded glass in the east wall above the altar. The Rose Window in the West wall was entirely of opalescent glass of different colors, and the center had a sky-blue background with a dove on a wing.

The Great Hurricane of 1938 carried away the steeple on the bell tower, separated the walls, and destroyed the beautiful Chancel Window. In 1965 the parish hall burned to the ground. A new hall was dedicated to the memory of the first rector and missionary, the Reverend Ebenezer Punderson Sr., in 1965. By 1969, the church and hall were connected, and the parking lot was expanded. 1989 marked the completion of an educational wing to Punderson Hall.

MJG 2014

MASHANTUCKET PEQUOT MUSEUM
And RESEARCH CENTER
1998
110 Pequot Trail, Mashantucket, CT 06338

http://www.pequotmuseum.org

Open May till November

This magnificent edifice of 308,000 square feet houses both permanent and temporary exhibits; one library for adults, another for children; a lecture hall: *The Gathering Space; The Pequot Café* that specializes in Native American food; *The Trading Post Gift Shop*; classrooms; administrative offices; conservation laboratories; and archives repositories. Its 185' tower provides breath taking views of the countryside. Two of its five levels are below ground.

Owned and operated by the Mashantucket Pequot Nation, the Museum features art, both ancient and modern, of the Pequot people, traditional crafts, videos and hands on displays of artifacts. The anthropology staff is committed to discovering and preserving evidence of this centuries-old culture. Multi-sensory dioramas, exhibits, and displays will enlighten both the scholar and the curious to the lifestyles of this ancient people.

For research, the library and archives are available free of charge. For their online catalogue visit: http://www.mpmrc.com. Advance notice for library research will allow the librarian to gather materials for you. Publications must be used at the library. Advance notice is necessary to access the archives, and staff will be available to aid you with your research.

Outreach programs are available, either online or by Museum representatives. These are ideal for schools or cultural groups who cannot visit the Museum.

Study their extensive website to learn more about outreach programs, schedules, tours, group visits, and special events, and visit them on Facebook [http://www.facebook.com/pequotmuseum] and at Pinterest [http://.pinterest.com/pequotmuseum].

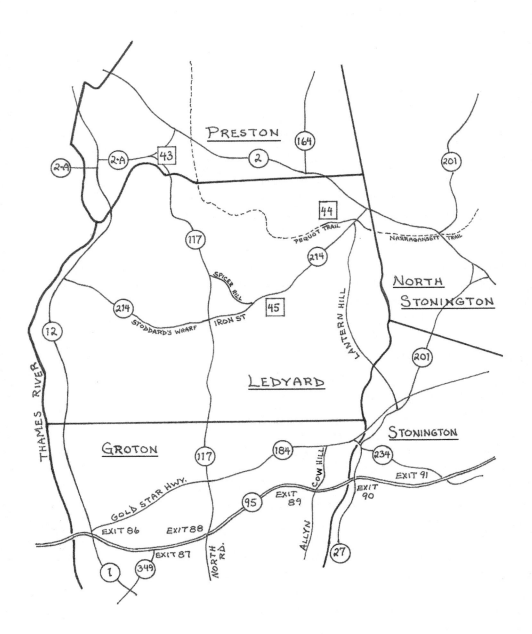

PRESTON

2-A 2·A 43 2 164 201

44

NORTH
STONINGTON

117 PEQUOT TRAIL NARRAGANSETT TRAIL

SPICER HILL 214 45

214 IRON ST. LANTERN HILL

12 STODDARD'S WHARF

THAMES RIVER

LEDYARD

201

GROTON 117 184 STONINGTON 234

COW HILL EXIT 91

GOLD STAR HWY. 95 EXIT 89 EXIT 90

EXIT 86 EXIT 88 ALLYN

EXIT 87

NORTH RD.

1 349 27

134

PRESTON

43   SAINT JAMES EPISCOPAL CHURCH

LEDYARD

44   MASHANTUCKET PEQUOT MUSEUM

45   UP & DOWN SAWMILL

- - - - - -   **Pequot/Narragansett hiking trail**

LEDYARD UP-DOWN SAWMILL
1877

172 Iron Street [CT Route 214] Ledyard, CT 06339

This sawmill was listed with the National Register of Historic places in 1972 as the Main Saw Mill, as the Main family last operated it from 1902 till 1935.

Israel Brown built this mill in 1877, and installed the sash vertical saw. 'Sash' describes the window-like frame in which the saw blade is mounted. The long straight blade is connected by a Pitman arm – such as drives locomotive wheels - to a heavy flywheel mounted horizontally. This is driven, through bevel gears at right angles, by a vertical shaft in a horizontal turbine driven by water power.

The eccentrically mounted Pitman arm provides this saw with a 24" stroke. The sawblade retracts slightly from its kerf on the return stroke, allowing the sawdust trapped between the teeth to fall away. An advancement pawl allows the carriage holding the log to advance from 1/8" to 1/2" per stroke, and the saw runs as rapidly as 100 strokes per minute when a full head of water can be provided. Up and down saws were outmoded with the introduction of circular saws around 1800, which, though they require more power, have many times more teeth per minute sawing the lumber; have steady, more gradual advance; and clear their chips.

The mill was idle from 1935 until 1966 when the town of Ledyard purchased it and began its restoration. Operated and maintained by volunteers from the Ledyard Historical Society, the mill is now open to the public during the summer and has occasional demonstrations. Visit them at http://www.ledyardsawmill.org

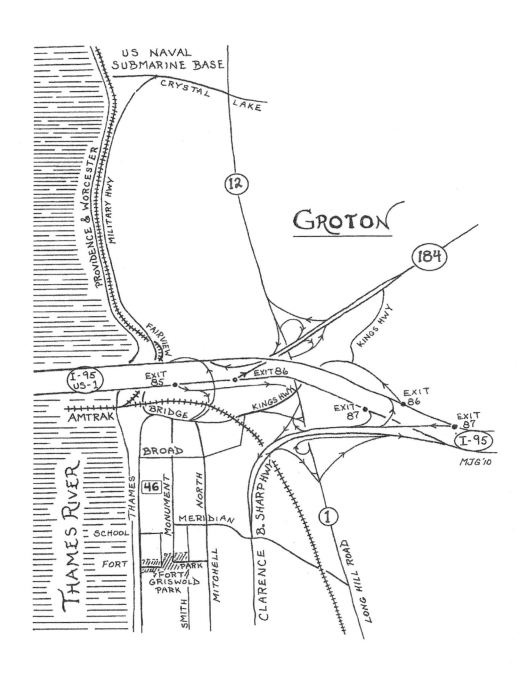

US NAVAL SUBMARINE BASE

CRYSTAL LAKE

PROVIDENCE & WORCESTER

MILITARY HWY

GROTON

12

184

FAIRVIEW

KINGS HWY

I-95 US-1

EXIT 85

EXIT 86

EXIT 86

EXIT 87

EXIT 87

I-95

KINGS HWY

AMTRAK

BRIDGE

MJG'10

THAMES RIVER

BROAD

THAMES

46

MONUMENT

NORTH

MERIDIAN

B. SHARP HWY

1

SCHOOL

FORT

PARK

FORT GRISWOLD PARK

MITCHELL

CLARENCE

LONG HILL ROAD

SMITH

46 AVERY-COPP HOUSE MUSEUM & THAMES RIVER HERITAGE PARK

140

AVERY-COPP HOUSE MUSEUM
Circa 1800
154 Thames Street, Groton, CT 06340

http://www.averycopphouse.org

The Avery- Copp House was built c.1800 by Rufus Avery for his two sons and their families. It was later sold to a cousin, Latham Avery - a successful merchant seaman.

One of his daughters, Mary Jane Avery Ramsdell, inherited the house and Victorianized it during the 1860's. The house was passed on to her niece, Betsey Avery Copp. Betsey and Belton Copp moved here in 1895 with their three children, Allyn, Emily, and Joe.

Joe Copp stayed on after the death of his parents in 1930, and kept the home virtually unchanged. When he died in 1991 at the age of 101, his nieces and nephews, who inherited the house, proposed that it be run as a museum in order to display and teach the lifestyles of former centuries. Though the family retains ownership of the three acres homestead, the Avery-Copp House is now open to the public. During the summer season they host Victorian teas, demonstrations of nineteenth century lifestyle, dramatic readings, and tours. The Carriage House now houses historical archives.

The **Thames River Heritage Park** project, now nearing completion, plans to link historic sites about the mouth of the Thames utilizing a water taxi to serve both new London and Groton. Their historic tours will include, in Groton, not only **the Avery-Copp House,** but also **Fort Griswold, [LM 96-97] The Submarine Force Museum,]LM 104-105] USS Nautilus,[LM 106-107] Bill Memorial Library, [LM 98-99]**and **The Ebenezer Avery House.** In New London it will include both **Hempsted Houses,[98-99] the Lyman Allyn Art Museum, [LM 80-81] the Nathan Hale Schoolhouse, Fort Trumbull, [LM 92-93] the National Coast Guard Museum [108-109]** and **Waterfront Park, the Customs House Maritime Museum, [LM 90-91]**Union **Station, [LM 86-87] Garde Arts, [LM 82-83]** and **the Shaw Mansion [104-105].**

For more information on Thames River Heritage Park:
http://www.thamesriverheritagepark.org

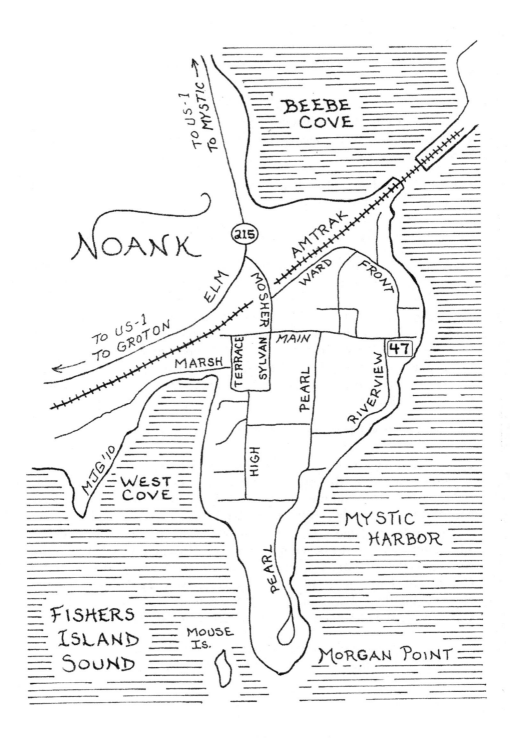

NOANK

BEEBE COVE

TO US-1 TO MYSTIC →

TO US-1 TO GROTON

215

47

ELM

MOSHER

WARD

FRONT

AMTRAK

MARSH

TERRACE

SYLVAN

MAIN

PEARL

RIVERVIEW

HIGH

MJG'10

WEST COVE

PEARL

MYSTIC HARBOR

FISHERS ISLAND SOUND

MOUSE Is.

MORGAN POINT

NOANK

47 LATHAM CHESTER STORE

LATHAM – CHESTER STORE
1840's
108 Main Street, Noank, CT, 06340

http://www.noankhistoricalsociety.org

This Late Greek Revival building was built in the 1840's by William Wilbur at the foot of what was often called, "Store Hill." Carson's Store [LM 110-111] stood at the summit; there was also a fish market, a ship's supply, and a grocer. The Post Office was at the front of this store – William Latham, Noank's first postmaster, bought the building in 1851. The front of the store was "The Lady's Store," and sold dry goods. The back of the store sold fishing equipment, and was "The Men's Store." Upstairs was "Latham's Hall" for assemblies and dances.

Latham died in 1878 and this country store had several owners until 1899 when Captain Daniel W. Chester bought it. The C. M. Chester & Co. Store also sold coal. In 1919, Chester sold the coal company to Dr. William M. Hill. In 1920, another building was moved behind the store to serve as the coal office. Hill's son, Claude, purchased the company and sold coal until the 1938 Hurricane, after which he moved the business to the Noank Depot.

In 1925, Hill's wife purchased the store and made it into apartments. Hill's daughter later converted the empty coal office to "The Chowder Kettle." During WW II it served as a canteen for Noank Shipyard workers. After the War it became "The Ship's Inn," under Alta Allen Codman.

The State purchased the buildings in 1962 for the UCONN marine biology Lab as an adjunct to the building next door that is now a shellfish hatchery. In 1987, the Noank Historical Society leased the buildings from the State. The Society collected $165,000 to restore the Latham – Chester Store, which now serves as a meeting, lecture, and exhibition hall. Members hang artwork there during their annual summer show. The building behind is presently undergoing renovation and will be used as a boat museum.

The Noank Historical Society Museum is housed in the former Grace Chapel at 17 Sylvan Street. See my article [LM 114-115]. Please see their website for a calendar of events.

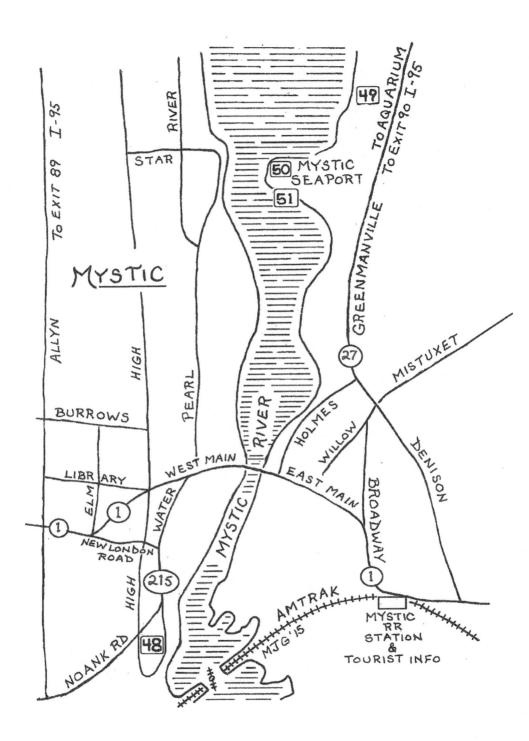

MYSTIC

CAPTAIN DANIEL PACKER INNE
1756
32 Water Street, Mystic CT, 06355

http://www.danielpacker.com

Captain Daniel Packer [1731-1825] was a captain during the Revolution. He was born in Groton, and married Hannah Burrows [1733 – 1801], also of Groton, in 1754. Her father, Hubbard, gave them some land on the west bank of the Mystic River. This compact Dutch Colonial was completed two years later. By 1769 Daniel ran a rope ferry connecting the New London Turnpike on the Groton shore to the Post Road in Stonington. A wharf and a store complimented the ferry, and the Packer Homestead also served as an inn. His son, Eldridge, was the first to build boats in Mystic, nearby the homestead. "Polly" was launched in 1784.

The last of the Packers, Mary Hannah Packer Keeler, occupied the house until her death in 1948. The Keelers continued to live there intermittently until the 1960's. Then it stood empty for several years – 18 rooms in disrepair and lacking in sanitation. The last resident, Charles Carroll Keeler, and his brother, Robert, planned to make it an inn. Their finances and Charles' poor health deterred them, and they sold the Homestead to Richard and Lulu Kiley in 1979. After four years of restoration, the house appeared much as it did 200 years earlier. Their daughter, Allison Kiley Nasin, now manages the inn.

For over 30 years, the Captain Daniel Packer Inne has served good food and drink, and has a loyal following. The tavern, downstairs, is informal, rustic, and friendly. The dining rooms, aloft, are subdued but stately. The food is gourmet, the service excellent, the wine list, extensive.

The National Register of Historic Places listed The Mystic River Historic District in 1979, which includes this inn.

As a footnote: Captain Daniel Packer's mother, Abigail Eldridge Packer, was the granddaughter of Captain Daniel Eldridge, who moved to Stonington from Rhode Island and, in 1704, built and dwelt in the Cape that I presently own in Old Mystic.

ELM GROVE CEMETERY
1854
197 Greenmanville Avenue [CT route 27], Mystic, CT 06355

The nineteenth century may have been the heyday of the American cemetery. The larger facilities were laid out as parks, with flowers, exotic trees & shrubs, rolled walks, tinkling streams, manicured lawns, & stone benches for resting or contemplating. People strolled about, picnicked, and admired the vast variety of lavish architecture and sculpture. Garlands of stone flowers, angels with flowing robes, and florid poetry graced the elaborate resting places of prominent citizens.

The earliest & most famous of these 'parks' was Mt. Auburn in Cambridge, Massachusetts, designed by the botanist, Jacob Bigelow, in 1831. Soon, replicas spread across the country. Cemeteries became a status symbol; they reflected the wealth & civic pride of the residents: both those interred & those left above to enjoy them. The term 'garden cemetery' sounded more pleasant than the stark 'graveyard.' Magnificent vaults, sepulchers, archways, & statuary graced these parks.

The Elm Grove Cemetery Association met in 1853 and raised $3800 through subscriptions to purchase twenty-two acres along the Stonington side of the Mystic River. A New York landscaper, N. B. Schubarth, designed this cemetery in the shape of an elm tree. The broad main path, named 'Elm' began at the gate, wound about the limits of the ground and returned to the gate. All paths were named after tree species. Elm Grove was dedicated July 11, 1854. The massive archway at the entrance, dedicated to the memory of Charles Henry Mallory, was completed in 1895 by the Westerly Granite Company. It spans 54 feet, is 32 feet tall, and 6 feet thick. The main arch is 20 feet wide.

In 1911, a marble chapel designed by James Gamble Rogers was dedicated to the memory of Thomas and Charlotte Greenman. A curator's house, a boat landing, a pond with a fountain, and extra acreage have been welcome additions.

SABINO
1908

Homeport – Mystic Seaport
75 Greenmanville Avenue [CT route 27], Mystic, CT 06355

http://www.mysticseaport.org

This 57' steamboat is the oldest wooden, coal fired steamboat still in active service in the U.S. She was built in East Boothbay, Maine by W. Irving Adams, and christened *Tourist*. She served as a ferry on the Damariscotta River; sank in 1918; was sold to become a ferry on the Kennebec River; and was rechristened Sabino after an Abenaki sagamore named *Sabenoa*. In 1927 she was sold once more to ferry passengers to islands in Casco Bay. By 1958, her service in Maine was done.

The Corbin family of Newburyport, MA restored *Sabino*, after which she served there on the Merrimac River as an excursion boat. She came to Mystic Seaport in 1974. She now serves as an excursion boat on the Mystic River and keeps busy during warm weather. In 1992 she was designated a National Historic Landmark.

Both railways and highways contributed to the obsolescence of steamboats, which, in turn, had proved more expeditious than horses or horse drawn vehicles. *Sabino* still utilizes her original two cylinder Paine compound steam engine, though her boiler was replaced in 1940. She was fitted with a conventional propeller rather than with less efficient paddle wheels, and averages 8 knots. Her captain, engineer, and two deckhands are responsible for transporting some 33,000 passengers per year.

I made this illustration from a photo I took of *Sabino* nearby the Seaport from my Whitehall pulling boat.

EMMA C. BERRY
1866

Home Port – Mystic Seaport
75 Greenmanville Avenue [CT route 27], Mystic, CT 06355

http://www.mysticseaport.org

Mystic Seaport is a premier museum and repository of historical ships, boats, documents, and nautical gear and paraphernalia. *Emma C. Berry* – designated a 'Noank Smack' - was designed by Robert Palmer, and built at the PalmerShipyard in Noank by master carpenter, James A. Latham. Noank is just downriver from Mystic Seaport and has a long tradition of boat and ship building; the Palmer Shipyard at one time was the largest builder of wooden vessels between New York and Boston. The Noank smack was a variety of fishing boat having a live well to keep her catch alive.

She was built as a sloop to the specifications of skipper John Henry Berry of Noank, who named her after his daughter. She is 45' 9" long with a beam of 14' 8".

In 1886 she was re-rigged as a schooner; taken to Maine in 1894; and powered with an auxiliary engine in 1916. She fished until 1924, and was then abandoned. In 1926 she began a new career as a coastal freighter between Gloucester, Portland, Rockland, and Jonesport. In 1931 she was restored by F. Slade Dale, and, in 1969, donated by him to Mystic Seaport. She was designated a National Historic Landmark in 1994.

My illustration derived from a photo I took of *Emma C. Berry* from my Whitehall pulling boat.

Once again sloop rigged, *Emma C. Berry* remains at the pier as a permanent display.

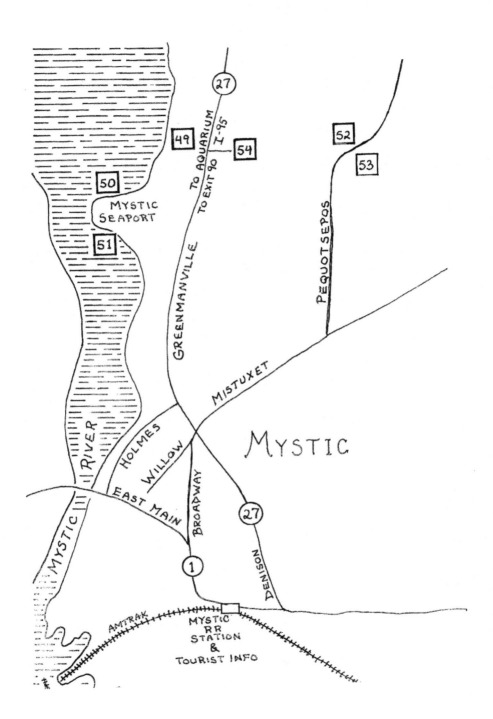

MYSTIC

PEQUOTSEPOS MANOR
AKA DENISON HOMESTEAD
1717
House museum
120 Pequotsepos Road, Mystic, CT 06355
htpp://www.denisonhomestead.org

DENISON PEQUOTSEPOS NATURE CENTER
109 Pequotsepos Road, Mystic, CT 06355
http://www.dpnc.org

COOGAN FARM NATURE AND HERITAGE CENTER
162 Greenmanville Avenue [CT route 27], Mystic, CT 06355
http://www.dpnc.org

The Denison Homestead owns over 160 acres of open space only minutes from downtown Mystic. The last Denison to own the homestead conceived the idea of founding the Denison Society – comprised of all living family members – to conserve the property. In 1930, Anne Borodell Denison Gates convened hundreds of the Denison family and explained her mission. The family have been the stewards of this estate ever since. In 1946 the Manor was restored by J. Frederick Kelly, with every room representing a different period in America's past. In 1979 the National Register of Historic Landmarks included the Denison Homestead. The Manor House is open for tours and events during the summer season.

The Denison Pequotsepos Nature Center, across the road, began as the Pequotsepos Wildlife Sanctuary in 1946. It became incorporated as the Denison Pequotsepos Nature Center in 1972. The DPNC & the Manor House are separate entities on the same property. There are 10 miles of trails, Nature walks, overnights, exhibits, classes, demonstrations, a museum, & gift shop. There are supervised programs for all ages. The DPNC is a federally licensed wildlife rehabilitation facility committed to saving ill or injured animals.

The DPNC, working with the Trust for Public Land, acquired 45 acres of the nearby Coogan Farm to form the Coogan Farm Nature and Heritage Center. This additional open space features more walking and biking trails with views of the Mystic River.

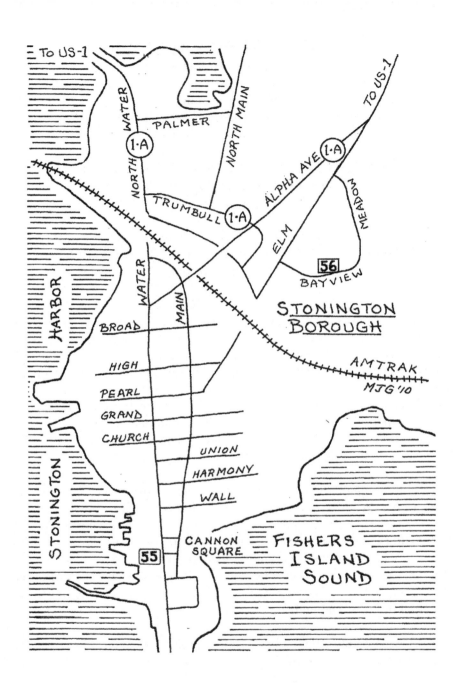

STONINGTON BOROUGH

MAURICE C. LA GRUA CENTER
2008
36 Water Street, Stonington, CT 06378

http://www.lagruacenter.org

Between 1849 and 1851 John F. Trumbull built a machine shop and a 60' x 30' foundry building by Stonington harbor. Trumbull Iron Works built cotton gins and steam engines on a small scale. More buildings were added and other businesses leased space. During the Civil War the Joslyn Firearms Company produced thousands of breech loading carbines for the Union cavalry.

By the late 1860's Trumbull, and Joslyn, were out of business. In 1876 the Atwood Machine Company, manufacturers of silk making equipment, purchased the building. They rebuilt the roof of the granite foundry and widened it from 30' to 41'. During the 1890's they built a new mill. A lack of innovation following the death of Eugene Attwood in 1926 doomed the Atwood Company. By the 1940's synthetic materials usurped the silk industry. By 1945 Atwood went out of business. Subsequent tenants of the mill included Emhart, Plax, and Monsanto. From 1982 until 2003 the building stood vacant – then fire gutted the mill.

Today the rebuilt mill is a condominium complex. The foundry, purchased and donated by Winifred La Grua in 2007, was named for her late husband - local photographer and hero of World War II, Maurice La Grua [1914 – 2005]. Fine art, music, lectures, readings, dance, book fairs, and more instill the La Grua Center with energy, cheer, awareness, and hope. Its patrons, directors, and audiences contribute enthusiastically to its present and its future. An intimate, light, and graceful space, the La Grua Center proves an inspiring place to visit.

VELVET MILL STUDIOS
Built 1888
22 Bayview Avenue, Stonington, CT 06378

http://www.thevelvetmill.com

A. Wimpfheimer & Bros. Inc began producing high quality velvet in this new building in1891. They wove, dyed, and finished their material with meticulous care – every step of the manufacturing process took place here with modern machinery designed by the Wimpfheimers, utilizing the craft of men and women who took pride in producing some of the best velvet in the world. This mill encouraged profit sharing and participative management. The result was an efficient business that lasted for over a century. At their zenith in the 1950's the mill ran 300 broad looms and employed 450 people.

By 1996 the company – now known as American Velvet but still directed by the Wimpfheimers – determined that the high cost of taxes, labor, and energy in Connecticut, and the low cost of imported velvet must be overcome by moving the company to Virginia. In 1996, Financial World magazine rated Connecticut 43rd of the 50 states based on its business climate. Alike most of New England's textile trade, American Velvet departed for ever.

By 2001, the first of a consortium of artists, crafters, and small businesses had taken up residence at the Velvet Mill. Today dozens of spaces are occupied by not only fine artists but also such diverse businesses as a micro-brewery, reflexologist, pastry shop, sign painter, and a psychotherapist. Open houses, concerts, flea markets, and farmers markets can all be discovered here. Office or studio spaces are available, as well as temporary space for larger functions. Come browse the Velvet Mill's eclectic milieu. A site map is available at their website.

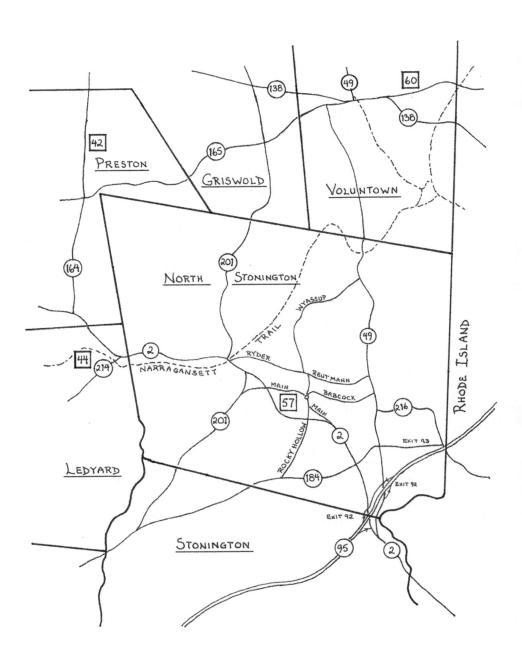

PRESTON

LEDYARD

NORTH STONINGTON

VOLUNTOWN

- - - - - -   Narragansett hiking trail

WHEELER LIBRARY
1901

101 North Main Street, North Stonington, CT, 06359

http://www.wheelerlibrary.org

The village of North Stonington Village benefited from the philanthropy of the Wheeler family - children of Major Dudley R. Wheeler. The Wheelers had prospered due to out-of-state investments in banking and iron furnaces. Miss Jennie Wheeler founded the school in memory of her brother Edgar H. Wheeler in 1889. Her brother, Henry Dwight Wheeler, endowed it.

The school occupied rented rooms from 1889 until 1901, when the present building was completed. The old Wheeler home became the principal's residence. The school had both boarding and day students; the girls and boys each had a dormitory on the campus. Tuition was free for day students from town. Rates for boarding students in 1914 were $350 per year, which included tuition, room, board, heat, electric light, and laundry.

As a secondary school, Wheeler offered five year college preparatory courses including Latin, French, algebra, geometry, and the sciences. Music and the arts were encouraged. There were also courses in agriculture, horticulture, the domestic sciences, and the domestic arts. This main building served as library and assembly hall, and contained laboratories and recitation rooms. By mid-century, secondary students attended Stonington High for a time, then in 1956 the new Wheeler High School opened.

This building now serves as North Stonington's elegant library. Built in the Richardson-Romanesque style, it features pink granite for window surrounds and belt courses, and blue-gray granite elsewhere. The round arched windows typify this style and the recessed front entryway with polished red granite columns and sentinel lions distinguish this classical edifice.

The National Register of Historic Places added the North Stonington Village District to its catalogue in 1983.

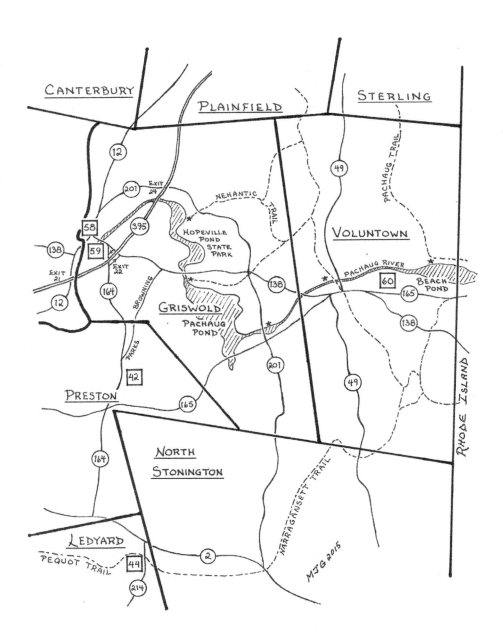

PRESTON

LEDYARD

GRISWOLD

VOLUNTOWN

SLATER LIBRARY
1884
FANNING ANNEX
1930
26 Main Street [CT route 12], Jewett City, CT 06351

https://sites.google.com/site/slaterlibrary

http://www.historicbuildingsct.com

This lovely small, Romanesque library was designed by Stephen Carpenter Earle [1839 – 1913] of Worcester, MA, whose masterpiece is the Slater Museum of Norwich [cover & page 1]. He is also remembered for designing Worcester's United Congregational Church [The Central Church], Pilgrim Congregational Church, Union Congregational Church, The Worcester Art Museum, Christ Church Cathedral in Springfield, MA, and the magnificent Old Chapel at UMASS, Amherst, MA. Many of the buildings he designed are on the National Register of Historic Places.

Previously, a tiny library in North Preston had closed in 1821, and auctioned off its collection of 372 books. In 1881, Dr. Daniel Coit of Pachaug – a village in Griswold – endowed a small library in the Coit Chapel, but this, too, proved inadequate. William Fox Slater [1815 – 1884], prosperous owner and manager of the nearby Slater cotton mill, left a fund to build and endow this library for his town. He set up his endowment to diminish year by year until the public – for whom it was intended – could totally support it. Though he died during its construction, his son, William Albert Slater, oversaw its completion. William also endowed the Slater Museum in Norwich in memory of his father.

It was built of granite from Milford, MA and trimmed in brownstone. The roof is of black slates and red, terra cotta tiles It cost $16,000 to construct. In 1927, local businessman, David Hale Fanning, left $75,000 to build an annex to the Slater. Cudworth & Thompson of Norwich designed this much needed addition, which opened in 1930. Downstairs is the children's library, on the main floor are housed thousands of books; upstairs is the quaint museum of the Griswold Historical Society.

The National Register of Historic Places listed the Slater in 2002.

SLATER MILL
1846
39 Wedgewood Drive, Jewett City, CT 06351

THE SLATER MILL SHOPS
http://www.theslatermill.com
COLLEGE MART FLEA MARKET
LEONE'S AUCTION GALLERY
http://www.collegemartfleamarket.com

Samuel Slater [1768-1835] was known as "The Father of the American Industrial Revolution." Born in England, he emigrated to Rhode Island, and immediately proved his expertise in setting up a cotton mill in Pawtucket with industrialist Moses Brown. His consummate knowledge of machinery and manufacturing processes led to his acquisition of mills in RI, MA, and CT. He and his brother, John, took over the ailing Jewett City Cotton Mfg. Co. in 1823. Renamed the Slater Company, it soon flourished. The present building on the Pachaug River was begun in 1846. Several later additions resulted in this present mill of 112,000 square feet that eventually employed 500 workers.

John Slater, the manager, was succeeded by his son, John Fox Slater, who made improvements to both machinery & the building. He also ran nearby Hopeville Mill, & backed the enormous Ponemah Mills in Taftville. He funded the Slater Library, endowed Norwich Free Academy, & received the Congressional Medal of Honor after giving $1,000,000 for educating emancipated slaves following the Civil War.

At his death in 1884 his son, William Albert Slater, assumed control. The Great Freshet of 1886 inundated the mill and necessitated extensive repairs, but, by the 1890's – the height of production – the Slater mill operated 19,000 spindles and 700 looms for producing cotton cloth.

William Albert Slater completed the Slater Library [page 172-173] begun by his father, and endowed the Slater Museum [cover & page 1] in his memory.

Today, the industrial revolution and the enormous textile mills that drove the economy of New England are all but forgotten. The Slater Mill now houses a multitude of small businesses, plus the College Mart Flea Market – open every Sunday of the year – featuring over 900 tables and over 150 vendors.

VOLUNTOWN PEACE TRUST
1962

CAMPBELL FARMHOUSE
Circa 1750

539 Beach Pond Road, [CT route 165] Voluntown, CT 06384

http://www.voluntownpeacetrust.org

In 1962, the 54 acre Campbell Farm was purchased by Mary Meigs, who turned the property over to Robert and Marjorie Swann, an activist couple who had been doing anti-militarism work as part of the *New England Committee for Nonviolent Action* (NECNVA). Mary Meigs was an artist and author; her friend, Barbara Deming, was a journalist. When the two traveled through India they were greatly influenced by the non-violent philosophy of Mohandas Ghandi. The two women became greatly involved in the NECNVA and the newly formed Voluntown Peace Trust.

The Farmhouse – built for local physician John Campbell – is a central chimney Colonial that is said to have been a stop on the Underground Railroad, as there were secret rooms built into the stonework of the basement. Today it is the focus of the VPT. The Peace Trust features talks, films, dialogues, conferences, and classes on peaceful coexistence and sustainability, as well as holistic healing sessions, nature walks, pot lucks, concerts, and retreats.

This statement from their website elucidates their philosophy:

"The Mission of the Voluntown Peace Trust is to serve as an educational, resource, and support center dedicated to non-violent social change and sustainable living. The Vision of the Voluntown Peace Trust is for a global society in which everyone lives free of violence, can truly participate, has a sustainable relationship with the earth, and whose basic needs are met."

Please stop by to visit and get involved!

CPSIA information can be obtained
at www.ICGtesting.com
Printed in the USA
LVOW04s0823171115

462852LV00004B/8/P